TIMBLE MAN

DIARIES OF A DALESMAN

TIMBLE MAN

DIARIES OF A DALESMAN

Selected and Edited
by
Ronald Harker

Cover by Stuart James

HENDON PUBLISHING : NELSON

First published in Great Britain, 1988
by
Hendon Publishing Co. Ltd.
Hendon Mill
Nelson
Lancashire

191

ISBN: 0 86067 110 0

Printed in Great Britain by
Fretwell & Cox Ltd.
Keighley
West Yorkshire

CONTENTS

I wish to thank Llewellyn Dickinson, grandson of the cousin of the diarist, who gave me access to the diaries; my nephew Peter Daggett for the illustrations, and Diana, Joy and the late John Holdsworth, without whose ready help this book would not have been published.

LIST OF ILLUSTRATIONS

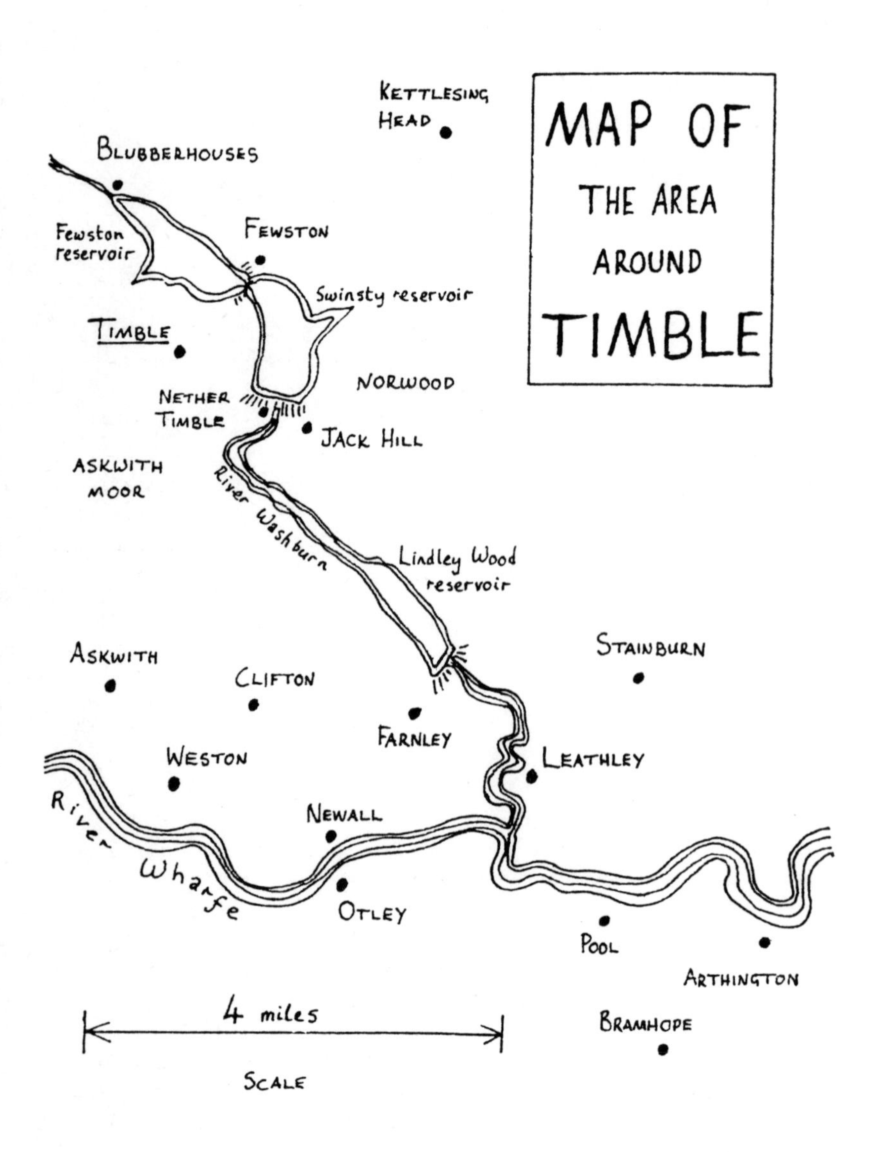
MAP OF
THE AREA
AROUND
TIMBLE
THORNTHWAITE
KETTLESING
HEAD
BLUBBERHOUSES
Fewston
reservoir
FEWSTON
Swinsty reservoir
TIMBLE
NORWOOD
NETHER
TIMBLE
JACK HILL
ASKWITH
MOOR
River Washburn
Lindley Wood
reservoir
ASKWITH
CLIFTON
STAINBURN
FARNLEY
WESTON
LEATHLEY
NEWALL
River Wharfe
OTLEY
POOL
ARTHINGTON
4 miles
BRAMHOPE
SCALE

INTRODUCTION

John Dickinson was born in 1844 at Timble. Great Timble and Little Timble, sometimes known as Timble Great and Nether Timble, are groups of houses and scattered farmsteads on a ridge of land running east and west on the southern slopes of the Washburn valley. The population of both villages in 1844 was about 200.

The valley is a minor Yorkshire dale. The Washburn, now interrupted by four reservoirs which it feeds, runs on as a tributary of the River Wharfe. The reservoirs were made to slake the thirst of Leeds. Fringed with deciduous and evergreen woodland they have settled into the landscape. If you stand with your back to the sun they shine as blue as the Mediterranean and look as natural as Norwegian lakes.

The Timbles are roughly nine miles south-west of Harrogate, six miles north-west of Otley, and twelve miles east of Skipton-in-Craven. They have no visual affinity with any of these towns: the inhabitants look out in all directions towards undulating hills, quilted pasture land and heather-coated moorland. Before the enclosure movements all this formed part of the ancient Forest of Knaresborough and was a feudal fee of the Archbishops of York. The Forest was enclosed in 1778. By that time the temporal power of the great prelates had evaporated, but they remained titular lords until 1837.

The scene changed little over the centuries. Except for better roads it was little different a hundred years later from what it had been in Dickinson's day. All change in the valley was slow and considered. A local historian wrote in the 1880s that the Timbles had not been distinguished for deeds of heroic virtue nor rendered notorious by crime; they possessed no great baronial halls, no battlefield of historic note, no noble monastic establishment, and so, he wrote, 'their history consists of a chronicle of small things'. Small things they may have been, but the valley bred stalwart men and long-enduring families: among them, the Dickinsons.

In 1504 when a lawsuit was brought to try to deprive Sir Robert Plompton of his patrimonial estates in Yorkshire, six Dickinsons of yeoman rank were witnesses. Oliver Dickinson was such a devoted servant of Sir Robert that when the knight ran into beggary and then imprisonment, Oliver accompanied his master and shared his

Highfield Farm, built by John Dickinson.

captivity. In the reign of Henry VIII William Dicconson farmed part of the King's Waste in the Forest of Knaresborough and in 1529 brought an action in the Duchy Court of Lancaster against the Prior of Bolton for trespass.

A John Dickinson was buried at the Washburn village of Fewston in 1658. In the following year Ann Dickinson married John Simpson, and William, a son of Thomas Dickinson, was baptised in the same place. In 1745 another John Dickinson married Mary Hardisty — and today Hardisty Hill will tell you where her family lived. John and Mary had two sons named John and Charles. This younger John also had two sons, one bearing his name and the other the name of his uncle, Charles. Charles married another Mary, a daughter of Joseph Holmes, who farmed at Timble. These two had a large family — another Charles, born in 1810; John, born in 1812; Elizabeth, 1814; Mary, 1816; Joseph, 1818; William, 1821; George, 1824; Martha, 1827; David, 1829; and another Mary (the first, it seems, having died in infancy), 1834. John, who was born in 1812 and died in 1875, was the father of my Timble Man.

The diaries came into my hands by chance. In the summer of 1980 my wife and I paid a visit to her three cousins, John, Diana and Joy Holdsworth, at Highfield Farm, Timble. In the drawing room after tea we sat beside a splendid fireplace of white marble veined in black. It was rather grand for a farmhouse and it occurred to me to ask the age of the sturdy stone house. Diana said it was exactly 102 years old. How could she be so precise about it? Well, a neighbour had recently lent them a diary which had been kept daily throughout the year 1878 by the man who built it. This was John Dickinson.

The diary was produced: a foolscap-size Blackwood's Shilling Scribbling Diary, interleaved with blotting paper, and prefacing its ruled calendar section with a mass of information on such matters as stamp duty, fees for deeds and wills, a calculating column for income tax at threepence in the pound, and postal services — one penny on inland letters and twelve deliveries daily in London starting at 7.30 a.m.

John Dickinson, like his father before him, was primarily a stone mason. He took into partnership his cousin William Dickinson when the business extended into building beyond Timble. In 1981 William's son Alec was 87 and living on the outskirts of Otley, and Alec's son Llewellyn, still following the family tradition as a builder, was living in Ilkley. He owned the diary, and in the hope of being able to copy interesting extracts from it, I drove the sixteen miles from my Wharfedale home to see him. He gave his consent readily, but said, 'You won't know it, but there are eighteen more volumes.'

They covered a period of thirty-four years, with some gaps — Dickinson stopped keeping a diary in some years, and other volumes have disappeared. But the nineteen preserved by Llewellyn, the last one going up to within a few days of the diarist's death in 1912, seemed to contain riches too abundant to be emasculated in a casual magazine article. So Llewellyn helped me to load them into the boot of my car and I spent the rest of the year reading them.

There were, as one would expect, periods of days or weeks when Dickinson found little to record beyond observation of the changing weather. There are teasing omissions of information. Some burning local issues are noted but not explained, and great happenings far beyond Timble rarely get more than brief and cryptic mention. Nevertheless, if the diaries, like the history of Timble itself, are only, as the historian put it, 'a chronicle of small things', they illumine as if in flickering starlight, a pattern of rural life in Yorkshire as one diligent and concerned man saw it in the last quarter of the nineteenth century and the first few years of the twentieth.

We meet him when he is 34 years of age, unmarried and living with his widowed mother. Three years earlier his father, then 63, went out to shoot wood pigeons and did not return. His wife and son, joined by a village search party, found him lying dead in a lane, his gun beside him, seemingly dead of a heart attack.

John is of modest stature, a small-boned man by his own description, weighing sometimes a little under 140 pounds and sometimes a little over. His face is heavily whiskered. He believes this strengthens his eyesight. He shaves only his chin. He fears for his chance of long survival whenever he suffers slight ailment.

Nevertheless he feels himself to be a good figure of a man and that throughout his life others think he looks younger than his years. His mother pampers him: on one occasion, for example, she sits up all night to make sure John gets a good sleep and yet wakens early enough next morning to join a village trip to the seaside. But he frequently makes a change from his mother's company, going off after the day's work to play cards with Uncle George, drink at the village inn, seek a sweetheart, or gossip at her cottage with his Aunt Mary — a habit which is to influence greatly his future life.

Like any countryman whose fortunes are at the mercy of a wayward climate, he makes close daily observation of the weather, rejoicing as a part-time farmer in a fine spell so long as it doesn't drift into drought and retard the growing grass, impatient as a builder of wild wet weather that impedes outdoor work. When winter wanes he can scarcely wait to hear birdsong and inhale the scent of wild flowers. A lyric impulse drives him into verse which only sometimes rimes and scans. He has a tender feeling for animals in pain, although the suffering of a hunted otter is obscured by his excitement in watching the hounds.

The quest for security is never far from his mind as it must have been with his fellow bread-winners before a Welfare State was dreamed of. He built his defences against poverty with what he ruefully concedes are too many irons in the fire. He spends money reluctantly, except on liquor, and joins a friendly society thrift club that will help to sustain him if he falls sick and cannot earn.

He is a sturdy walker, probably less from choice than because there was no other way to travel out of the valley and over the fields and moors — until increasing prosperity and ambitious concern for his place in what he begins to call 'the social scale' enables him to buy a horse and trap. He eats well enough of a limited range of basic food. His meat in younger days is mainly pork sparerib because one of his multiplying occupations is buying and salting fat pigs and selling hams and flitches of bacon.

Sexual potency excites him and although he assuages it from time to time in the natural way he cannot reconcile it with sufficient affection for his 'sweethearts' to contemplate taking any of them for a wife. He is both vain and cautious about this. He convinces himself that many a local girl would be glad to marry him, but, bent on securing only an ideal partner, he cannot discern one among his conquests.

In early manhood he is a dedicated — or, at any rate, a diligent — worshipper; ecumenical too, for he attends the Anglican church on Sunday mornings, chapel — Methodist or Congregational — in the afternoons, and parish church again in the evenings. He is sure he was born for better things, and has no doubt that had he had the advantages which he sees the rich provide for their children, he could have risen to eminence in almost any professional or artistic walk of life. Coupled with his steady, if modest, material progress, this brings him to diminishing respect for the quality of his fellow villagers. His attitude is enhanced with his range of reading. He reads Thackeray, Dickens, Carlyle, Macauley, Tom Paine, Charlotte Brontë, Shakespeare. His vocabulary improves through the years, although he has not mastered syntax at school and uses no punctuation.

His interest in happenings beyond the valley expands a little through a more regular reading of the county newspapers. It is enough to make him worry about rebellion in the colonies and to prompt him to part with five shillings — more than five pounds in modern money — and walk fourteen miles and make a train journey to and from Leeds to hear Gladstone speak. But his references to stirring political and social events are scanty: the hanging of the notorious Charles Peace in Armley jail; the arrest of the wife-murderer Dr Crippen (although he could not guess that the crime would be remembered a century later only because radio was used for the first time to trap a killer); the great Jack Johnson's fight for the heavyweight boxing championship of the world; Louis Bleriot's historic 37-minute flight across the English Channel; the Afghan, Zulu and Boer wars. The few hints in the local newspapers of military blunders in all three of these theatres of warfare disturb only slightly his abounding faith in the invincible courage of British soldiery and his belief in the world-civilising mission of the British people.

Yet he is well aware that he is living in an age of tremendous technological and political change; the coming of the motor car, and hard on its tyres, the flying machines; strikes by workers which curb for a time the boom in railway travel. He feels it is in keeping with his material success to condemn incipient socialism, yet it worries his innate conservatism that the King seems to be enjoying grouse shooting on neighbouring moors irresponsibly when trouble in the coalfields is threatening a breakdown in national industry. And he has something like furtive, almost guilty, acclaim for the Asquith Government's readiness to create 250 Liberal peers to check the power of the House of Lords to thwart the will of the House of Commons.

In middle age John Dickinson was strongly influenced by two men. Both were born in the Washburn valley near Timble, and both found fame and fortune in the United States of America. Dickinson admired self-made men and these were paragons.

One of them was Robinson Gill. His maternal ancestors were wealthy yeomen living at Swinsty Hall. In 1815 one of the Robinson girls married William Gill, a Nidderdale man who carried on a 200-year-old family tradition as a stone mason. The Gills had five sons. Four of them emigrated to America and followed their father's trade there. Robinson was the youngest of them. He had been a pupil in a dame school in the nearby village of West End and then at Timble, and in 1851 when he was 22 and not yet out of his apprenticeship, he joined his brothers in America as a journeyman mason. He progressed to the ownership of two large stone yards on the banks of the Hudson and East rivers in New York, employing up to 300 men. He also became president of two New York banks: a solid citizen.

Like many successful expatriates before and after his time Robinson Gill wanted to register his achievements by some memorial on his native heath. He settled on giving Timble a building that would be a social centre, a library and a free school. It cost £861 8*s*. and the builder was John Dickinson, who also became one of the first trustees.

Robinson Gill provided the library with £100 worth of books bought in Leeds, and he endowed the building with £2,000 which he asked to be invested in land to yield an income of £60 a year. All began well, and at the opening ceremony in 1892, the second hero in Dickinson's life delivered a keynote address. The speaker was the Reverend Robert Collyer, a friend of Gill's. Collyer spent the first fourteen years of his life in the Washburn valley and when the family moved to the town of Otley he became a blacksmith there. It was as a blacksmith and at the age of 36 that he emigrated to America in 1850 and continued to ply his craft for the next ten years. Collyer was a voracious reader and buyer of books and at the end of ten years he left his smithy and was exercising a rare gift for language in flamboyant oratory as a Unitarian minister in Chicago. On trips back to England he stayed with John Dickinson and it may be assumed that it was Collyer who inspired the diarist to begin reading great books. It may also be assumed that Dickinson sought to emulate Gill, even if the most fleeting and surprising sign of this was his chosen honeymoon journey, for Dickinson at last plunged into matrimony — although the reader of the diaries may well suspect that he was steered into this at Aunt Mary's.

Robinson Gill died in 1897. The news, cabled from America and carried to Timble, was not the whole shock. It unmasked another. The family fortunes had declined. It was discovered that the endowment money for the village hall had not been invested in land, as Gill at one time requested or intended. Instead it had been turned into shares in one of his enterprises — the Denver paper mill. This was now foundering. Dr Collyer accepted power of attorney. He managed to sell the paper mill bonds for a small sum, but the revenue for the library, and hall, dried up. The school closed in 1904. The hall, dedicated by name to Gill's maternal forebears, still serves as a centre for the village's social gatherings, although the depleted library had become a handful of damp-rotted books by the

1980s, and a large oil painting of the donor, a gift from his Huddersfield-born wife in 1890, hung in melancholy isolation. The old school desks were rusted and piled in the basement.

With advancing years Dickinson gradually discarded the more strenuous of his occupations — masonry, farming and pork salting — and accumulated more clerkly duties. The irons in the fire that he once thought too many became even more numerous. He had been a paraffin salesman, a tea seller, an agent for selling manure, a trader in hay, an insurance agent. In place of some of these he now became a waywarden concerned with the state of local highways, an inspector of plans and buildings for the local authority, overseer for the Board of Guardians, official for the periodic distribution and collection of census papers, a rate collector, a vaccination officer, and parish councillor. He retained the job of registrar of births and deaths for three townships (which he had inherited from his father). As well as being a trustee of the Robinson Memorial Hall he was secretary and grand master of the village thrift club which bore the title of Lodge of the City of Refuge Friendly Society, a branch of the Honourable Order of the Peaceful Dove. The club doled out help to members who fell on hard times under a code of 57 rules to which John Dickinson was a signatory. When he himself fell sick he did not hesitate to put in a claim on club funds. In 1893 there were 128 members of the Lodge and on Whit Tuesdays at the annual meeting of members they ate a free dinner at the Timble Inn and then marched in procession to a service at Fewston Church, led by a visiting brass band.

At the same time that his combined sources of income grew (and he did not despise £7 a year from one source), his church-going fell off and his questioning of orthodox belief and spiritual guidance increased. He also alienated himself from the youthful excesses he once enjoyed — denouncing overt love-making and riotous drinking. He moved his home to a large house on the fringe of Otley and his familiarity with farming folk withered as he began to enjoy more sophisticated town company. His enthusiasm for walking declined too, not merely because of diminished vigour so much as because of a waxing enthusiasm for train travel. He memorises all the departure and arrival times of local services which were then more numerous than they are today.

His sober regard for his wife Fanny, who is fourteen years younger than he, is touched with the growing realisation that her miscarriages and the slight mental backwardness of their only child, probably arises from the consanguinity of Fanny and himself, for she is Aunt Mary's daughter.

Surprisingly, his early premonitions of a short life for himself and his recurrent gloomy speculations on the hereafter, have vanished from his diary entries at the onset of his final illness. He is active in his work and hopeful about his health when he has fewer than four days to live.

The last entries in the last diary are by Fanny herself recording her husband's last hours and the prolonging of her distress in an unexpected interruption of her husband's funeral.

In 1981 you could still visit his homes in Timble and the outskirts of Otley, see the cottages of his Uncle George and Aunt Mary and the farmstead where jilted Emma lived and died. His own mark on the Washburn valley is in a few other houses and barns, their builder forgotten were it not for the diaries he kept, but which, it seems, he never expected others to read.

Ronald Harker

John Dickinson's birthplace in Timble.

1878

Tuesday, January 1. Working at Messrs Chas. and Geo. Holmes new house at Timble. I have contracted the masons work and I have already dressed most of the stones. It is fine open weather. I am in fair hopes of a happy and prosperous year if my health holds good.

Thursday, January 3. Today we drew the lines for the foundations of Holmes new house and all is going on smoothly. Joe Holmes is doing the digging. Fine weather without frost. I am staying in my house on evenings now . . . Tonight I am in good spirits. Just got a glass of Irish whisky hot. Going to bed directly, 10 o'clock.

Sunday, January 20. After dinner took walk to Timble Ghyll. Interview with Caroline Spence, then on to church in the evening on look out for a sweetheart with view to wife. One brandy at Public, then home to bed at 10.30.

Monday, January 28. Got ready to attend School Board meeting. A thaw set in and all was wet and slushy so we adjourned to Mr Ward's at Hopper Lane inn. Got part brandy and had tea. Called at Magic Lantern performance at the Huts.* After at Aunt Mary's till 11 p.m., then home, mother worrying what had got me. Freezing keen again.

Monday, February 4. Worked hard at Holmes house walling. Got a bad cold and had onion porridge to supper. To bed by 10.30. Rather tired.

Saturday, February 9. Walling at house up to 4 p.m., then washed and shaved and dressed smartly to attend Watch Club in evening. Got half tipsy. Had a restless night on that ale, but in fair hopes and spirits. Must have a sweetheart.

Tuesday, February 12. Up by 7. Breakfast and to work walling at Holmes house. Fixed kitchen window bottom and back door bottom jambs and binders. I am hearty and strong at present. Read

*The Huts housed work teams building Swinsty Reservoir. Building began in 1871 and was finished in 1887.

todays *Yorkshire Post* and from all accounts England can hardly be expected to keep from entering upon war with Russia. What the consequences may be we can hardly tell. May God preserve us as a nation and save me as a poor weak member of the Commonwealth.

The crisis subsided. At the Congress of Berlin the following summer Russia was fobbed off with a piece of Rumania. Britain got the right to occupy Cyprus in return for guaranteeing Asiatic Turkey against possible Russian attack.

Saturday, March 16. Not working today. Dressed up very smart. Took vaccination notices to several houses and Huts about Fewston. Saw my late sweetheart, E. Beecroft this evening. Feel sorry that we never had any connection.

Tuesday, March 19. Up at 6.30 and did a bit of digging in the garden till 8 then breakfast and went to work at the house. Squared things up ready for more walling when the floor gets on. Had a glass of ale or two about 4 o'clock with Charles Flesher who is poorly. Graved the garden up to dusk then shaved and washed but felt tired. It is most beautiful weather seed time nearly over and farm prospects look well.

Friday, March 22. At Otley. A bad day. Got on miserable. No business and all gloomy I am fairly down and see no way out of all my troubles, only by waiting and living down certain false rumours that have got abroad respecting me and a certain young woman whom I have courted some time ago.

Wednesday, March 27. Very keen frost. Lifted window tops on house floor and had some mulled ale. Playing cards in evening. Long to have someone to love. Stars shining like Christmas.

Sunday, March 31. Chief talk of the village is about E. Beecroft being with child. Changes occur. What will follow no one can tell. All is mystery what with war rumours and domestic scandals all seems upset.

Monday, April 1. A wild snowy day. Registered a birth at waterworks Huts on Swinsty Moor. In good health and spirits and hopes to come out pretty smart during the Spring and get a sweetheart . . . I feel rather alone on account of all my old companions having got married. Shall try this Spring . . . Hewed keystones for window tops at Holmes house and put the year 1878 on one of them. Jas. Lister walls inside and Joe Holmes and Will Wood labour and we work hard.

Saturday, April 20. Up by 6. Walked to Otley by 9. Took train for Leeds. Made arrangements with Leeds firm to supply nitrate of soda. Had my head examined by a phrenologist. Mutton chops and tea at Gapton's restaurant. A thoroughly wet day. All flooded coming home. Well tired, but at Watch Club after and to bed by 10.30.

Thursday, May 9. Sorting out slate, timber levelling in afternoon. Mother off to Guiseley so I am alone to do cooking. Feel very miserable when I come in to a meal and nothing ready. I have 4 masons who lodge at the public house hewing for me at the house. I want to push it on fast. I feel a great want of something to stay my wanderings and unsettled purpose. My great want seems to be a loving wife.

Wednesday, May 29. Slating at Holmes house till 3 then dressed up pretty smart and went to sports on Swinsty Moor in connection with waterworks. Many hundreds of people there. Foot races, tug-of-war, sack race, bell run, wheelbarrow race, and race for females. Good knife-and-fork tea was provided. I passed off pretty fair but did not make any progress in the female way. Hopes to do better during the summer.

Tuesday, June 3. Completed fixing tabling at Holmes house. Cut gutters for leading chimneys. Emma Beecroft has confessed to David Holmes that she is in the family way to Joe Lister. Joe denies paternity and so there will be a rare scandal in which my name will be used pretty freely. Such is life.

Thursday, June 13. Flagging cellar at Holmes house and fixed stone shelves round cellar. Navvy at waterworks cut his throat with a carving knife. Nearly killed his wife before he did it.

Thursday, June 20. Got tipsy at Robert Fishers. Came home soon after 10 to bed. Brought a hedgehog home. It knocked about wonderful during the night.

Wednesday, July 3. Down at Pool. A fair day. Got four threepenny whiskys and several bitter ales. Registered four births and one death. One of the births occurred at Caley Lodge on the road and the mother was removed to the workhouse where she arrived when I was there.

Thursday, July 4. Finished fixtures setting at Holmes house and removed all tools and made out my bill which amounts to £102 1*s* 3*d*. which I hope to draw tomorrow.

Friday, July 5. Joe Holmes and I tried the ghyll for fish and got a little fry at Uncle George's. Talk is about Emma Beecroft who is reported to have got a child today. A fine boy they say and nobody is its father.

Monday, July 15. All busy with haytime. Only I am idle doing nothing all day. Went down to Swinsty in the afternoon and spent an hour or two with Polly Clarke at Holmeses. She was moderate kind and of course I cuddled her thoroughly.

Monday, July 29. Timble Feast. Rather a wet morning but got into a remarkably nice day in the afternoon. Mrs. Dawson came on a visit. A good many navvies present in the evening. Three open stalls and two Frenchmen with a dancing bear. Altogether a lively stir. A lot of us repaired to Uncle George's granary after 10 p.m. and dancing and singing continued up to 5 o'clock next morning.

Wednesday, August 7. Off to Pool by 7. Called on Holmeses at Swinsty. Cuddled Polly Clarke. A wet walk to Pool. Sat two hours at the White Hart. Got three whiskys hot. Rode up to Otley with a party of yeomanry cavalry who had been at Harrogate. Called at George Spences and cuddled Polly there. Quite a kissing day I have had.

Thursday, August 8. Off to William Simpsons of Norwood to work building him a new mistal. Took meat with me for all the week and staied all night. A fine day and worked hard and got on well. Worked till it was dark and to bed by 10. I slept with William Simpson on three feather beds but didn't sleep well.

Friday, August 16. At Otley. Walked both ways. Had a summons delivered to me to appear as a witness in Emma Beecrofts affiliation case with Joe Lister. Home by 7 and then went to Beecrofts to register birth of Emmas child. All is looking upon an eventful footing. Who would think that I should be called as a witness?

Friday, August 23. At Otley. Off by 7. Rode with Jonathan Spence. E. Beecroft had Joe Lister up to pay to her child. I was summoned on her behalf. An excitable day, but I was not called upon. The result was an order for ten shilling a week. Had an interview with Emma previous to the trial and she was loving as ever and gave me a loving kiss. A wet day. Rode back with Jonathan.

Sunday, September 10. Dressing stoops for garden wall at Holmes house. A very warm day. Dropped work about 5, washed, shaved and dressed up very smart and went down to hear the Rev. Robt. Collyer give his lecture in the Board School on Fewston in 1620 and Edward Fairfax (local poet, translator of Tasso's 'Jerusalem Delivered'). The place was well filled with the leading inhabitants of the parish. Mr. Ashley, the Vicar presided. The lecture was a masterpiece of pathos and eloquence and must have cost an immense amount of pain and labour to get the facts and ideas together. A beautiful fine night. Called at Aunt Mary's and staid till 11.

Sunday, September 15. A wild wet and windy day. Got a few nuts before noon in Timble Ghyll. I had agreed with E.B. to meet her if it was fine, but I suppose it was so wild that she couldn't get out and I was fool enough to go over. What a fool I am to begin with her again. But fate somehow makes me hanker after her to work my ruin. I feel also certain however that Providence has stepped in to save us from the worst in connection with this unfortunate evil.

Tuesday, September 17. A wild and windy day so not at work. Shaved and dressed before breakfast and wrote out bills up to noon. At Uncle George's and then public house and then in the evening down at Aunt Mary's. Feels in better health and spirits than common today. Also a better flow of wit if I may so speak. That is my intellect feels free and unclouded. We have such times occasionally in our lives which comes in upon us very often like a gleam of sunshine in a dark sky. Such is life. We are here battling with the realities of daily existence. How little we know about ourselves. We are taught to think that we have something about us that is immortal and it is a grand hope. But then when we look at Creation in all its immensity and think of the illimitable extent of space and time with the systems and suns and worlds governed by the same unchangeable laws we may well think, what is man? I cannot deny the existence of a supreme Being who must be good and all-powerful and it is not consistent with unerring wisdom to make human beings with these hopes and aspirations only to be annihilated after death. Therefore I incline to the belief that we have a destiny beyond the grave. Let us hope it may be a happy one.

Tuesday, September 24. To bed by 9. Mother sat up to get me off soon. Up at 3 a.m. Got ready by 4 and off to Darley Station (five miles away) in company with several young persons from here. Train left Darley at 6.18 and we were there in good time. An exceedingly long train and crowded. Arrived at Scarborough about 11 and did all the sights including the aquarium, Castle Hill, and promenaded with my lady companions and altogether spent a very enjoyable day though I was suffering from a bad cold. Rode home in a second class carriage and had a most loving companion with me. Got home thoroughly tired and to bed and slept soundly.

> *Travel by steam railway was booming in 1878 creating a public appetite for cheap day trips. The Yorkshire historian Henry Schroeder recorded that in August and the first two weeks of September in 1844, the year of Dickinson's birth, 60,000 people visited Liverpool, York and Hull, all from Leeds, Sheffield, Wakefield and some industrial villages. On the morning of Thursday, 12 September, he says, a train of 240 carriages drawn and propelled by nine powerful engines took 6,600 passengers from Leeds to Hull and back at a reduced fare of two shillings, third class.*

Friday, September 27. A showery morning. Went down to Aunt Mary's at White Crag in the forenoon and talked with Fanny about her trouble at Scarborough. In the afternoon worked at Holmeses garden wall. E.B. came and I showed her round the house and cuddled her as usual, and then did what I suppose had not been done before in the house since it was built. We both were, I believe, proud in a sense at being the first to take part there in such an enormous event.

Sunday, September 29. At church in the morning. Met E.B. at 2. Then an old repetition with which I was disgusted. I am very foolish to be in it but I couldn't help the temptation. Left her about 4 o'clock. To church in the evening. Very dark and murky. Came up with a girl that I love.

Monday, September 30. My head aches and I don't feel right but in fair spirits on the whole. Hopes to be again successful amongst the females and I hope I may get a loving wife out of it. We cannot tell what awaits us but there is no harm in hoping for a good thing.

Tuesday, October 1. At Uncle George's playing cards from 8 to 12 a.m. on a wild wet morning. Afternoon with women at Holmeses house. They are cleaning it. Amongst them Miss Clarke and I had pleasant romps occasionally. Met E.B. at 8. Found her loving but no time to stop with me.

Thursday, October 3. Working at Holmeses garden wall. Walked over to meet E.B. in evening. Saw her but she could not stay as her folks watch her so tight. I feel glad it is so as the thing is fairly alarming.

Sunday, October 6. Church in morning. Chapel afternoon. Church again. Nothing particular. In fair spirits upon the whole though bothered about females.

Saturday, November 2. Off by 7. Joe Holmes with me. To Brown Bank Chapel to put chimney pot on. Joe and I called at Lister Holmeses and got a quantity of spirits and in coming home I lost Joe. David his brother went to look for him in the evening and found him near Mr Moorhouses barn where he must have been laid four or five hours. He had fallen. Dead drunk of course. I was rather tipsy but travelled without showing it much. At Watch Club at night.

Friday, November 6. A very cold north wind. Snow came in the afternoon. Went to Aunt Mary's and had tea there. Staied till 7 o'clock. I hardly know what I go there for unless it is to look at Fanny.

Tuesday, November 12. A regular stormy winterly morning. Snow drifting and frosty. Still I went to work to make a vault for the burial of Mrs Thos. Simpson of Norwood. Had tea at Masons and a few glasses and got home about 7. My birthday. Am 34 years old and really must look for a wife.

Friday, November 22. Otley Statutes [day for hiring labourers] Very cold. Not so many people as I have seen at Statutes. Pretty well looked upon and I passed off moderate well I think. I hope by steady effort and earnest purpose to get a wife by and by. Did not get at all drunk.

Saturday, December 14. The storm continues. Went to William

Simpsons and bought a fat pig. From there to Mr Marstons at White Crag and bought a pig and two hams. Then to Aunt Mary's and arranged to have another pig and so did a fair amount of business. Price sixpence per pound for pigs, sevenpence halfpenny a pound for hams. At Watch Club supper at night. About 40 partook of supper and jolly drink after.

Wednesday, December 25. The boys were about by break of day shouting greetings. The waterworks band came with their music in the forenoon. I was at home all day. Only went out to see E.B. in the evening. I spent an hour in the house from 8 o'clock and then played on my concertina for a jovial party at Fred Ingles till 12. Part warmed ale stirring the old course again. So it is in life. To bed partly affected by the ale.

Saturday, December 28. Dull and misty day. A shooting match came off in the afternoon at Timble. Miss Clarke gave a party in the evening and a lot of the swells of the neighbourhood were there. We had a very pleasant party rollicking with the girls, drinking whisky and playing games of all sorts. Left about 12.30. Came up with John Beecroft and Margaret. A very wet night. To bed not tight.

Tuesday, December 31. Rose at 8 a.m. Washed and shaved and felt quite lithe and clean. Making up registration and rain gauge accounts and taking stock of what I am worth. Upon the whole I have had a fairly prosperous year though my income is less and my expenditure bigger than last year. And in addition to that bad trade has cost me a loss of £50 in mill shares . . .

I am deeply sensible of many shortcomings during the past 12 months. Though I have done a good portion of work I have neglected to cultivate my mental qualities and the year's result in that line makes but a poor figure . . .
I have bothered a good deal after the ladies during the year but not one step have I taken likely to result in getting to myself a wife. It has all been idle flirtation if not something worse. Plenty of girls of fair social position would have me I think but somehow they all seem to come short of what I hope to have in a wife. One only I have an eye upon and I doubt whether she would have me. But I must go on hoping and probably Providence which has always behaved like a kind friend to me may provide a decent body cut and shaped ready for my hand. With regard to my social standing I have reasons to

hope that I figure better than I did twelve months ago though I am still rather wanting in reserve and stability. The general trade of the country was hardly ever known to be so bad as at present. Great distress prevails in all the manufacturing centres and large towns and the future is all doubt and uncertainty. But it has been beautifully said that the darkest hour is just before the dawn of day. We will hope that we have seen the worst and if the good time is coming I trust that God in His good providence will arm me with fortitude and courage to dash to the front and gain that success which my ambition always led me to think was my due.

1879

The year commences with general depression in trade such as has not been known in my time. Much suffering and want prevail on all hands, which is aggravated by the severe winter. The frost for the past fortnight was hardly ever known to be so severe, but a thaw has cleared it off for the New Year.

Speaking politically things are very unsettled. We are at present engaged with a war with the Ameer of Afghanistan in India. And the conditions of the peace lately made betwixt Russia and Turkey at Berlin give cause for general uneasiness. Some other of our African dependencies are also in a state of rebellion, and what with one trouble and another old England is likely to have plenty to do to steer the vessel of state during the coming year.

The campaign against the Ameer was Britain's third Afghan war in which Sir Frederick (later Lord) Roberts led punitive expeditions to quell anti-British demonstrations, in the course of which he made his celebrated march from Kabul to Kandahar — 320 miles in 23 days with 10,000 men. The Treaty of Berlin aimed at a balance in south-eastern Europe acceptable to the great Powers. It revised the Treaty of San Stefano (March 1878) which ended the Russo–Turkish war of 1877–8 and in spite of the uneasiness mentioned by Dickinson the main lines of the settlement lasted for 30 years. In the Zulu war of 1879 British forces under Lord Chelmsford blundered in seeking to destroy the army of King Cetewayo which was menacing the Transvaal, but succeeded with the help of 10,000 reinforcements led by Sir Garnet Wolseley.

Wednesday, January 1. Got ready and off to Pool by 8.30. A fine morning it having frozen during the night and made it clean walking. Lindley Wood reservoir covered with ice which the late severe storm put on eight or nine inches thick. Looked in at the workhouse regarding deaths. They had a treat of rabbits. Called on George Spence and had two glasses of beer and some rabbit pie. Saw E.B. at six o'clock, then home and busy writing.

Friday, January 3. At Otley market. Rode both ways with Jonathan Spence. Good sale for pigs offal. Sparerib 8¾*d* a pound, leaves [a fatty layer of pork from which lard is rendered] 8½*d*. Bought a pair of hams at 7*d* per pound. Sold a flitch and had a fair business day. Home by 8 then at Aunt Mary's till 11. A most beautiful moonlight night and freezing very keen.

Sunday, January 5. Went to Blubberhouses to meet E.B. Came home with her. We mutually agreed to give up keeping company as I had no intention of making her my wife. The poor girl cried and I felt very sorry for her. But what can one do? She is ruined.

Monday, January 6. Stormy yet very keen frost. At home all day writing and jobbing about. At Aunt Mary's from 5 till 10. Home in a fine moonlight walk. The world to me looks bright and enjoyable at present. Weighed myself. Weight 9st. 11½lbs.

Thursday, January 9. Got 4 fat pigs in and busy all afternoon. Uncle George's in evening playing cards. Special services are being held nightly at our chapel but I don't feel to take an interest. I cannot reconcile it with my ideas of what is proper. May God give me light to see what I ought to do.

Tuesday, January 21. Up at 9. Washed and shaved and feels quite gentlemanly just doing nothing at all.

Wednesday, January 22. Hung 4 pigs. Gossiped about. Read Burns poems to mother for an hour in the evening.

Friday, February 14. At Otley. Called at Dr Duckworths and told him I was rather deaf. He took an instrument and looked into my ear and told me he could cure me in a few minutes. So I set him to work and when he had done I could hear as well as ever. It was the wax had dried. Rode home with Jno. Spence. He was rather drunk and quite foolish.

Tuesday, February 25. Charles Peace hung at Armley Gaol this morning at 8 o'clock. A noted criminal.

Sunday, March 9. A fine dry day. Went to church and came back by Aunt Mary's and staied awhile. Mother off to bed. I sat musing awhile. Somewhat depressed. Life seems to be made up of unfulfilled hopes. How bright are our hopes but how poor and empty seem all the past days of our life.

Tuesday, March 25. A very keen frost and a terribly cold east wind. In the afternoon I was digging out stones in the field known as Town End. About 9 p.m. I went down to the tavern. This March 25 used to be a great day at Timble when the eatage of the lanes was let. Great excitement and differences took place. Now things are changed. But we had a right jolly stir for an hour, playing and dancing.

Saturday, March 29. A very rough rude company of navvies and disreputable females at public house. It is to be hoped the works [building reservoir] will soon be over and these evil days done away with.

Friday, April 11. About home in the forenoon and working in the fields. Then at waterworks paying for manure. Away for a few hours in the evening on a courting expedition but something had occurred to prevent the dear creature getting out to see me so I had to stand for an hour out in the cold and no one came to cheer me.

Tuesday, April 15. When this interminable weather of winter will end we cannot say. No signs as yet. Got three glasses of whisky at the public. In fair spirits but must have a wife and then I suppose I shall be happy as is customary for poor humanity to be. Read Tom Paines works. Sowed some onions and set potatoes.

Sunday, April 27. At home all day till about five o'clock when I went round by Spink Helm and on by the waterworks and met E.B. at the site of her former residence and — poor girl — she told me that she had had a miscarry to me. I really must give her up finally as to go with her now is a disgrace to us both.

Sunday, May 4. At home all day till evening, then went about 6 to meet E.B. down the moor side. Spent an hour pleasantly with her and came home. Had five glasses of whisky at the Public after. Rather stirred with them.

Sunday, May 18. At home all forenoon. Met E.B. about 1 o'clock down at the plantation going to Swinsty Hall. Staied with her till 4 — And we had a regular repetition of old ways. Poor girl. I wonder what will be her destiny. I am foolish but I am tempted to see her again after not seeing her for a week or two.

Thursday, May 22. Brother Chas. brought me two cows today so I am now a keeper of livestock.

Sunday, May 25. Off to church then at home till 6 when I went round by Four Lane Ends and down by Spink Helm and up by Beecrofts allotment to meet E.B. She came out and we spent an agreeable hour, but Joe Holmes caught us in a field corner so there will be a noise about it.

Friday, June 13. Working at Mrs Atkinsons place. Very warm day. Met E.B. down at Swinsty about 1.30. Spent a pleasant hour and enjoyed the fun but I really must give it up. Nothing but ruin about it. Worked till after 8. George Lister had a cow shot by order of the superintendent of police to bury six feet deep in quicklime.

Friday, June 27. A wet morning. No work. Mr Dickinson from Stainburn brought me four hams. In afternoon met E.B. in the Green Lane going to Blubberhouses. We again mutually agreed to give up keeping company as we have been doing, but I fear there will be further trouble about it. I hope that I may get thoroughly clear of her this time as we destroy the happiness of each other.

Friday, July 4. At Otley where I sold a calving cow for £25 10*s*. Got part brandy and walked out with Nelly Beck up the Old Chevin. Nelly is a pleasant, sociable red-haired girl.

Wednesday, July 9. A thunderstorm in the afternoon and very heavy rain. I fixed the joists for laying board over the mistal at our place . . . Our pet dog Nancy which we have had for nine years was in a state which made existence a misery to herself and a nuisance to us so we sorrowfully considered to have her put away this evening about 9 o'clock. Joseph Dickinson hung her. Poor old Nance.

Monday, July 28. A fine morning. Spread hay swaths in the afternoon and the day was a good hay day and Timble Feast had a bit of sunshine. One or two novelties appeared in the way of catching pennies. One was a swing boat which was well patronised. The other was a boxing place which was also fairly patronised. I was on foot in the evening passing off fairly successful among the girls though I am getting rather past the bloom of youth. Still, they think it too good a chance to let slip.

Tuesday, July 29. Up by 7. Andrew and I twined Town End hay, then I jobbed about in the afternoon. We carted the whole of it finishing about 9 o'clock. Not very strong at present. I can't eat as I ought to do to stand hard work but still I am in fair health on the whole. Fiddling and dancing at the public tonight. Lively stirring all day at the public, quoit playing, etc. It is fine weather and all are at the utmost stretch with the hay in the first summer weather we have had.

Wednesday, August 6. Off to Knaresborough with Wm. Norse and his wife. Paid £200 on mortgage of farm near Dob Park. No work at the hay. Most corn hardly begun shooting. Back home by 7. Saw E.B. after dusk. She tells me she is in a bad state through me but I cannot think of marrying her. What the consequence will be I cannot forsee.

Wednesday, August 13. Got Crooked Close into three pikes yesterday. A beautiful hay day and led four loads out of Field Sike after tea. Worked till dark and commenced loading hay today by 8 o'clock. Got three loads by about 11 when rain fell. Somewhat unsettled in mind about nothing in particular. Most of all a sort of empty delusion about young girls. I am an old madling to bother with young girls only in their teens yet, but my heart is all ablaze if I see a pretty young girl and so I go on from year to year.

Sunday, August 31. Teaching at Sunday School. After tea went to Green Lane, Blubberhouses to meet E.B. Came back by waterworks wall. Rather a pleasant time only she says she is in the family way to me. Cannot say what will be the end of it.

Dickinson and his mother are moving to another house and he is making repairs or additions — he speaks of fixing window stones 'at own house', getting 'ready for roof', fixing a chimney, and flagging — but whether all this is for a rented house or his own new property he doesn't reveal.

Saturday, November 8. Flitting. Got all removed by 2 o'clock. Things fit very well. I think we shall be more comfortable here. Quite busy what with cattle and pigs and other matters. Rather seedy today on account of yesterday's conduct. Got more whisky than was good for me but not drunk. Club night. All favourable apparently and by God's blessing and energy on my part I hope to do well in future.

Thursday, November 13. Still getting things fit up. Preparing for going to Liberal Demonstration tomorrow. Churned for first time at new home today. Pretty good yield of butter.

Friday, November 14. All ready by 8.30 to start for Otley where I took the 11 o'clock train for Leeds to join in the great Liberal Demonstration. Took luncheon at the Town Hall at 2 p.m. and heard Mr Forster and other eminent men make speeches.

> *W. E. Forster, a Dorset-born man who prospered in textiles in Bradford and became the town's M.P. piloted the Education Act of 1870 which recognized education as a public service. Locally-elected school boards — Dickinson was a member of Fewston School Board — were empowered to establish schools maintained in part by local rates. School attendance became compulsory in 1880, and all fees in elementary schools were abolished in 1891.*

About 5 p.m. I left the Town Hall for Messrs Fowlers large shed where the evening meeting was to be held. It was a wonderful sight to see upwards of 20,000 people all in one building. The Duke of Argyle presided and made a long speech, but the meeting being so vast he could not be very well heard. Left Leeds about 11 p.m. for Guiseley where I staied the night [at his brother's home].

Monday, November 17. Busy all day about pigs and cows. Got three fat pigs which I intend killing and salting. Not yet settled in house but things are mending every day and we hope to be comfortable by and by.

Tuesday, November 18. Met E.B. about 7. She is getting stout. She says I am the father. What will be the end I don't see.

Monday, December 22. Saw E.B. in evening. She tells me she had a miscarry on Saturday evening last. So I am clear and I trust that I may be able to give that accursed connection up. However I am to meet her tomorrow noon to talk matters over.

Tuesday, December 23. Did not see E.B. as she did not come, from what cause I don't know. Fine weather. Must have a sweetheart of some kind or a wife perhaps will be better. This raking about does me no good neither in character nor in health.

Christmas Day. The boys shouting by 7 o'clock. Got up and did the cattle. Went to Mr Snows at Thornthwaite. Got beer there and staied two hours. A pleasant walk home in the moonlight and a brisk frost. Very quiet village. At Fred Ingles till 3 next morning. Weighed myself. 9st 13lbs.

Wednesday, December 31. A very rough day. I am full of reflections about the follies of my past life, but I suppose I shall do much as I have done before and fall into the old ruts again. But we will hope that I may get into a better way and get a decent wife and then I expect that I shall be more settled and lead a more moral life.

And so the year ends: It has brought about a few changes affecting my daily life. I have removed to a fresh house and got to be a farmer. Upon the whole I have had a prosperous year, financially having saved about £80. I have been well employed at mason work all the year and that has done very well for me.
I cannot think that my present condition and mode of life is the best for my peace and happiness. I am always in a state of excitement about females and my conduct with respect to that has been very foolish and immoral. I have kept up a connection with a person that I ought to have given up long ago and the result of it has been anxiety throughout the year and dishonour to both of us. Though not quite clear of her influence I hope to give her up entirely before long. May God give me the courage and will to give up evil habits and live a better life in 1880.

Whether or not John Dickinson gave up what he calls evil habits and lived a better life in 1880 cannot now be known. His diary for 1880 has been lost. But it becomes clear from the diary for 1881 that he has not been required to give up his association with Emma. By 1881 she is dead.

1881

I enter upon the New Year full of reflections. I am painfully impressed with a sense of my many shortcomings during the past twelve months.

Amongst other evils I have taken more alcohol than is good for me, and although I have not allowed its effects to master me, nor am I in any danger of getting a liking for it, still I have given way too much to the habit of taking glass after glass when away from home.

Then again my brain has been in a very idiotic state about the girls. Some fair young charmer or other has constantly been enslaving my fancy and I have frequently gone off very silly and contrary to what I knew was proper and right for a man of my age and position. One cannot help having certain passions and in the matter of females I am a fool because I am led astray when the light of my own intelligence points out plainly that the end of it all can be no good. I guess the best thing for me to do is get a wife.

My motto for 1881 is less alcohol less idle visionary excitement about the girls and less expenditure but more energy and industry, more solid and serious effort to get a suitable wife, more reserve more restraint more charity and more true manliness. May God help me to carry out at least some of these reforms.

Monday, January 3. Up by 8. Milked and went to John Umplebys of Meagill and bought a fat pig at 8*s* 4*d* per stone of 14lbs head and feet off. Back home by 2. Taking no alcohol yet this year. Feels better for it. At the old club. Got two glasses of raspberry brandy. Home and to bed.

Wednesday, January 5. Off to Pool by 8. Registered two deaths and one birth. The people down at Pool are chiefly poor working people who are dependent on the paper mill and stone quarry and those trades are very bad just now. But there are several gentlemens residences occupied by retired tradesmen from Leeds.

Thou cold bleak month of frost and snow
How keenly doth thy north winds blow
God bless the poor whose lot is cast
Exposed to thy relentless blast
And may the rich give of their store
To warm and feed the needy poor

Thursday, January 6. Mother and I hung flitches and hams off seven pigs. Very busy with that up to noon. Then Isaac Wilson of Widra came with a fat pig and I had to cut it up and salt it. And what with one thing and another I have been very busy all day. Got a letter from Cousin William Dickinson who is in Australia. He talks of coming back as it is only a poor country.

Saturday, January 8. We had a party or supper in the evening. Roast sparerib and guests Aunt Mary and her husband Joseph Holmes, Uncle George and James Lister, cousins Fanny Procter and Patty Dickinson, and David Wilkinson dropped in. After supper we had a nice quiet stir with games of whist. Held out till 2 in the morning and then quietly dispersed. These little diversions from the ordinary routine of life are necessary in as much as they conduce to an interchange of friendly sentiments and smooth the hard angles of everyday life. We cannot be happy without others sharing the blessing with us.

Monday, January 10. A keen frost. Up by 8 and milked. Busy writing out a new Poor Rate at eightpence in the pound. Then at Uncle George's cuddling Patty. She is a fine fat sansi girl . . .

I try to be merry and happy and gay
And sorrows dark clouds I defy
My duties are light through the short winters day
At night in warm blankets I lie.

Wednesday, January 12. Joseph Holmes and I arrived at Mr Yeadons at Arthington just in time for dinner which we enjoyed then sat for an hour drinking whisky with Mr Yeadon. Miss Yeadon played the piano and sang very sweetly. Took 3.30 train to Otley. Heavy snow shower as we came from Weston Moor, Timble Great.

Thursday, January 13. Up by 8. Perhaps 10 minutes past. Milked, foddered, swept snow off gates. Fetched a lot of water for mother. Read a little in a newspaper which the Rev. Robt. Collyer sent me from New York. Gave cows a little oil cake and more hay. Keen frost and like to continue.

An easy pleasant life I lead
With time to study and to read
Provisions plenty coals galore
What man on earth requires more?

Monday, January 17. Storm still severe. After doing the cattle I assisted in weighing Uncle George's pig. She weighed 41 stones 1lb. James Lister had a hard job cutting her up as the bacon was frozen like ice.

The lassies with their ever-changing fancies
Into my heart cut like so many lances
Just now I'm smitten by a pretty wench
Which drives me off the path of common sense
What can I do? My heart is just like tinder
With passion burns until its like a cinder

Tuesday, January 18. A shame to say it but I'm getting slothful and idle, in fact almost hopeless. The fresh hope and fiery ambition of my younger days is almost dead and lately I've begun to feel I am getting old. I suppose I am not strong constitutionally and I hardly expect to be of long life.

Cold blows the wind
Gloom fills my mind
Past memories sad
Future looks bad

But a voice says cheer
Spring is soon here
When birds will sing
And primroses spring

Sweet Spring hasten here
And with thy tunes cheer

Friday, January 21. Pretty busy day at Otley. Frost as keen as ever. Wharfe frozen over and hundreds skating on the ice. Somewhat busy about census matters. Walked both ways. Very tired on getting home about 7. To bed by 10 and slept soundly.

The storm continues keen and cold
Crows and magpies getting bold
They pick about the haunt of man
Poor things they are so thin and wan

Monday, January 24. Keen frost continues. Up by 8 and milked. Then hung three fat pigs sides and hams and had the hanging capacity of the house tested to its full extent. Pretty good health and I enjoy the storm and frost in a quiet way. A thick mist overhangs the country and not a breath of wind stirs. The trees are beautifully fretted with frost work and look very romantic and wonderful.

Tuesday, January 25. Jobbing about the house and barn and paying occasional visits to neighbours houses and jogging along, talking scandal and getting into trouble and out of it, and bothering about girls and feeling jealous and getting better of it and eating and drinking and feeling gleams of hope and happiness and glums of blackness and despair.

Friday, January 28. Off to Otley by 9 and pretty comfortably employed with pleasant duties for a few hours. Cousin David Dickinson and I staied till 8 o'clock flirting about among the lassies. Got home a little after 10 in a sober condition. Very dark night and we had a little difficulty along the road.

The night was dark the road was bad
As we across the moors did steer
With hope we through the mist did pad
And storm and rain we did not fear

My body is indolent. My mind and conscience are energetic and active, so I defer work till the last moment.

Away with your noise about teetotal joys
I cannot support your dull cause
If no whisky we get we shall all be dull boys
And our Parliament needn't make laws

Thursday, February 10. Dull sloppy frosty misty dirty rainy curious weather. Winter with its cold hand laid upon the hills is still darting his icy breath upon our pleasant vale. Labour is stagnant. People are huddled round the fires spinning yarns of days gone by.

A few years ago when labour was brisk
And workmen had much their own way
Men would carelessly spend without running a risk
Of being short of cash on some rainy day
Now the balance is changed and the labourers gone down
To the level of povertys brink
And the cry of distress may be heard in the town
Caused chiefly by taking strong drink.

Friday, February 11. At Otley. Pretty busy day. Got several glasses of whisky more than was good for me. Staied at George Spences till 10 o'clock. Very moonlight night. Came home with Ephraim Wilson, of West End, James Lister, Joseph Dickinson of Timble and Dick Holmes of Fewston, a very select company.

Getting bits of comfort from many little things
My harp of life contains full half a hundred strings
And if a string should break and run me off the line
I can always find some comfort among the forty-nine

Sunday, February 27. Still it snows. At home all day. Had fire in the parlour. Read Goldsmith's beautiful little story, *The Vicar of Wakefield.* In bed by 11.

Tuesday, March 1. Still very keen frost. Snow showers throughout the day. No sign of abatement and things are kept back. No outdoor work going off. Uncle George had a cow died today. Wrote to Cousin William in Australia. I long for the genial beauty of Spring.

Snow snow snow
Farmers cannot plough
Frost frost frost
All nearly lost.

Thursday, March 3. As rough a day as we have had all winter. Not a note from a bird has yet been heard in the ghyll and Nature looks dead. In the evening I took my fiddle to Uncle George's and we were singing and playing for a few hours. As cold a night as ever blew.

Saturday, March 6. Snow lying a foot deep. It rained most of the day which turned into ice and the trees are coated with ice to a thickness of near an inch. Towards night the weight of the ice on the boughs began to be too much for them to bear and the havoc of boughs breaking off was terrible.

> Difficulty and doubt beset my path
> I'm getting thin as any lath
> Bright hope seems dead within my heart
> And life seems hardly worth a fart

Tuesday, March 15. A most beautiful Spring morning at last. The birds sang, cocks crew and hens cackled and all Nature danced for joy. I went down to Leathley to meet several enumerators on census business. Came back through Stainburn. Cast amorous eyes at a buxom girl. Got home about 7. In pretty fair spirits towards evening.

Monday, March 21. Spent a very idle day indulging in sensual desires and neglecting true honest work which alone can make life bright and cheerful. Mother off to Samuel Philips of Snowden taking a shroud for Sam who died on Sunday last. He had been like a madman for a week.

> Death, we heard thy name but know thee not
> None know thee but the silent solemn dead

Friday, April 8. At Otley. A very complicated day. First I got a few glasses and then chatted with the lassies until it got to dusk and there I was with David Dickinson and Cag Holmes taking things quite jolly and comfortable. Got home about 10 somewhat affected by the whisky and beer.

These women do keep me in a most ungracious state of agitation. A pair of rosy cheeks with sparkling eyes and pearly teeth have got possession of what little I possess of mind and heart and so I stay and stay, held by their magic spell until the stars begin to peep . . .

Thursday, April 14. The country has got dressed in a spanking new suit of green tinted here and there with modest daisies and fringed with primroses. The birds have begun to sing once more and a general feeling of joy and hopefulness right around. At Otley. A busy day but not very fast money-making. I am dabbling in a good many little businesses all of which bring in something and I have serious thoughts of giving up masons work.

Wednesday, April 20. William Dickinson my cousin and William

Croft arrived safely home from Australia. They left here last June and after much trouble and disappointment they decided to return home. They are both thinner and no doubt wiser men. Probably it will do them good. The worst is they have spent most of their money.

> And so it is some fail and some succeed
> Some cannot headway make howe'er they push their greed
> It seems the best to work with patient will
> And not be off too fast like Croft and Will

Sunday, April 24. Church in the evening. Subject: death of the Earl of Beaconsfield. Mr Ashley preached it in his usual original style and the congregation was good.

> *Disraeli, 1804–1881, died a year after his second ministry.*

Wednesday, May 11. At George Holmes in evening. Mr Holmes, the new Board schoolmaster was there playing the piano and George and I fiddled. Pleasant concert.

Friday, May 17. Down at George Holmeses in the evening. The new schoolmaster was there playing the piano and George and I played our fiddles. We made a capital chord. I am very fond of musick. I think that I have a natural gift for musick and if I had been properly trained in my youth I might have come out rather superior to most persons. As it is I can play the fiddle the concertina and tin whistle just decently.

Wednesday, May 25. Working about doing nothing, the day being wet and wild. Did some writing at home. This quiet life hardly suits me but as I get older I feel more stayed and settled. I have no need to work very hard under present circumstances as I make nearly £2 a week independent of mason work. The sources of my income are from registration (of births and deaths for the Fewston district of 13 villages covering 25,000 acres), bacon salting, rain guaging under Leeds Corporation, manure agency, insurance agency, overseers work and several small items which drop in incidentally. Upon the whole I am a busy man and ought to be able to live without rough mason work.

I will pack up my tools and live a life of ease
And try to get along with duties that will please
My fancy and my health which are both a little crazy
And indulge in leisure time though some may call me lazy
But I hope by looking out for some easy jobs that pay
To make a litle headway against a rainy day

Thursday, June 2. Went down into Timble ghyll after dinner while the sun was hot and had a good bathe and wash in a large hole in what is called the Plonk Close, a place where farmers have washed their sheep this season. I enjoyed it very much. Afterwards I came up the stream and caught three trout and had them made ready for supper and enjoyed it very well.

Friday, June 3. Rode to Otley in Chas Holmes cart with three calves. New potatoes selling at threepence a pound. Fine ones. Didn't buy any however. Pretty busy day but somehow felt a kind of depression. A pretty girl's smile would have done as much good as anything but she was not there to smile and so I was miserable as I deserve to be for the manner I have treated confiding girls in the past. But I will be more true in future if I get the love and confidence of another dear charmer. Home by 8. At Inn till 10. Busy writing till 12.

Tuesday, June 7. After milking got ready for the club. The Guiseley Brass Band of Musick arrived about 10. There were about 80 club men present and it was very busy at the Timble Inn. We walked (in procession) to Fewston Church and made a good show. Club meeting in the evening and then a dance which was carried on with great spirit up to 10 o'clock then all turned out. Afterwards several mischievous young fellows committed several depredations such as upsetting Jack Sheppard's spice stall, ducking a chimney sweep in the watering trough and putting the club flag into the tarn. And so the day ended.

Friday, July 8. Off to Otley by 8 and there before 10. An active day. I flirted and talked with farmers' daughters and staied drinking and blowing on with regular ranting times until 10 o'clock at night. Then I quietly started off for Timble, a distance of six miles up Newall Carr and over the moors and through the ghyll and got home footsore and tired by just 12 o'clock. To bed and slept soundly.

Timble Inn.

But before he dropped off his fancy wandered and he added:

One morning in July I took a little walk
And with a maiden fair I had a little talk
Her teeth were pearly white and her lips were rosy red
And I wished with all my heart I had her in my bed

The first sign appears that Dickinson has begun to educate himself. The impulse almost certainly came from Robert Collyer, the blacksmith turned Unitarian minister in New York, whom the diarist admired.

Wednesday, July 20. Very quiet in the village. Read *Jane Eyre* through yesterday and today. The characters are well drawn and the work shows evidence of a peculiar but powerful and dramatic genius in the author. One feels better able to face the difficulties of life after reading such a work.

Dickinson was three years old when Jane Eyre was published. By the time he came across it Charlotte Brontë had been dead for twenty-six years at the age of 39.

Thursday, July 21. Haytime. Commenced mowing grass this morning. King Grange mows for me. I was up by 4.30. A most beautiful morning, and everybody active. I spread swaths most of the day. King mew all the Town Field . . . All matters have to give way to the all-absorbing question of hay-time. A good deal of ale is drunk and the work goes on joyously enough. The scythe is more in use than usual this season. I have let my bit of mowing to King Grange and the poor fellow works very hard though he is getting rather old for hard work. Besides he has only one hand. He lost the right hand through an accident with a thrashing machine.

Friday, July 29. At Otley busy buying good things for Timble Feast. Bought 17lbs of inlift beef and other etceteras. Had one of those days when by some unaccountable means things seem favourable. I spent no small amount of time talking to a pretty young female under the White Horse balcony. I suppose it will end in nothing but talk, but we both seemed interested and it was all well and pleasant. Back home by 8. I walked both ways. Then at the Inn after getting home.

Wednesday, August 3. Up by 7. Very wet wild morning. Started off to Pool. Got wet going as the grass hung over the footpaths and wet my legs very badly. Arrived at Pool about 11. Got two brandies there, then registered two births. Staied in Otley a good while and got several bottles of stout. Called in here and there to look at certain females. I am in danger of going astray among the forbidden fruit. But one has these fiery passions and they cannot be kept completely in check. I think I shall have to get married and then I shall be more settled. Perhaps, and perhaps not.

In November, just after Martinmas, the Otley Statutes Hirings were held in the market place when men and farmers met and agreed terms for a year's *work. The transactions were sealed with a 'God's Penny'. In 1882 all-round men could command £25 to £30 for one year, food and board found; second-class men cost between £18 and £25; strong youths £14 to £16; boys £10 to £14; females of experience £18 to £30; younger ones £15; girls £8 to £10.* Conditions were often hard.*

Monday, August 15. Up by 7 and off to Otley with Aunt Mary and Tom her son who had a county court trial at the county court today. Tom had lived servant with a Charles Holmes of Hawksworth and left before his term was up. So Charles would not pay him anything. Tom summonsed him but the decision of the court was against Tom and the result was that he had to pay about £1 and lose all his wages. That seemed very hard for poor Tom as he had to be up by 4 o'clock every morning.

Monday, August 22. All busy pursuing the phantom pleasure. Some drinking at the public houses where a pianist and singers engaged to amuse visitors to Guiseley Feast. Charles, my brother and I had a drive round by Yeadon and Carlton in the forenoon. After tea we all repaired to Yeadon where all the whirligigs and fun was held. Hundreds of young men and women were gathered on Pennyfool Hill where the hubbub and excitement was intense. All the public houses were crowded . . . In Guiseley all next day. Spent several hours at the Red Lion where there was singing and playing and other amusements going off with great spirit. I got only about three glasses of beer all day so my enjoyment was not of a violent character. I was much amused with the evident determination of everybody to drink and spend to the uttermost farthing. There was a large number of tramp singers and beggars of various description about the town and the demand for coppers from those and the boys was difficult to satisfy. However we kept merry and had an excellent time.

Wednesday, August 24. Up at 5. Went to Otley station to see the Scarborough trip off. About 1,500 went by it and the sight was quite animating. Cuddled a servant girl before breakfast at Guiseley and was caught by the housekeeper who however said nothing further about it. Public houses a little more quiet as the money was getting

* *This Little Town of Otley,* by Harold Walker, 1974

scarcer. In the evening had a walk to Menston with a young woman who was very loving and obliging. In fact she said she had no objection to marry me. I should not think of marrying her so the affair will go no further unless she wants me after a while. Guiseley Feast is a time when three days holiday are kept. The working folk spend their money freely and get through it by about Wednesday afternoon. Some go off to the spas, Morecambe or Scarborough. The wealthier class enjoy themselves in a more exclusive way.

Thursday, September 1. Part bother with the cattle just now. Thinks farming a poor business and I should have been better off without it . . . We have a lot of extra work and anxiety and there is very little to pay for it. My mother has rather more work than I think good, but she is used to work and I don't think she is hurt with it yet . . . The prospect is very gloomy for farmers all round . . . I am much bothered about my cattle as they are picking their calves and take a lot of looking after. Affairs all round are very bad and nobody seems to have any hope left. The wind is north and a good deal of rain is falling regularly.

Friday, September 9. Pretty busy day in Otley. Wombwell's Menagerie came into town about 12 o'clock. There was quite a block of traffic at Black Horse corner. They had 50 horses, also two elephants and several camels yoked into harness. I went into the menagerie at 2 o'clock and was very much interested.

Wednesday, September 21. Brother Charles and Thomas Procter came for hams. They got 20, weight 520 lbs at 10½*d* per pound. It came on heavy thunder rain in the afternoon making a great swim. The schoolmaster in a dying state all afternoon. Mother was the only person who durst stay with him. The rest all frightened of the infection. The poor fellow expired about 7 o'clock. Mother laid him out assisted by a girl who had come from Barnsley to see him. Village in an alarmed state as there are other cases of fever.

The schoolmaster died of typhoid. In 1850 Timble villagers built open courses and some stone drains to bring water from a spring two miles away into stone troughs in the village. Thirty years later it was found that the water became polluted on its journey. In 1884 water was brought into filter and storage tanks and thence in cast iron pipes to houses and *farms, the villagers being rated per house and per head of cattle. Dickinson became superintendent of the system.* The villagers locked the dead schoolmaster in his house for fear the infection would spread still further.*

Saturday, September 24. A hearse from Otley arrived in the village soon after 7. With some difficulty parties were got to put the poor schoolmaster into a coffin. Then two females, one his sister and the other his sweetheart, cried loud and bitterly. Soon the hearse drove off with the corpse to Sessay near Thirsk where his parents reside.

Friday, September 30. Off to Otley by 8.30. Attended Court House at 11 with jury list. Also gave evidence against Edward Newbould whom I had summoned to appear to show cause why he should not have his child Annie Elizabeth vaccinated. An order was made for him to vaccinate within a month or take the course of the law. Marketing afterwards: a very warm close day.

Now comes information about the fate of Emma Beecroft. In this, the last reference he ever makes to the ill-starred love affair, he does not mention her name.

Thursday, October 6. Went to work at Beecrofts at Ridge Top. Impressed while working with remembrance of courting incidents which occurred years ago at this same Ridge Top, when I used to pop over from Timble on evenings to meet a sweet pretty girl who said she loved me. I too loved her in a way, but I could not take her for my wife. After a short life of misfortune the poor girl died of a consumption hastened no doubt by the results of her indiscretions. I regret the part I had in working her ruin, because I always had a tender regard for her, but we lured each other on and the result was trouble and vexation. May the Lord forgive us such wicked acts.

Saturday, October 8. Heard the Right Honourable W. E. Gladstone, Prime Minister of England, at Leeds. Up by 6, off by 7, got to Otley to take the 9.19 train to Leeds. Looked round Leeds for a few hours. Saw the Premier arrive at the Town Hall. I repaired to

* *History of the Timbles and Snowden,* William Grainge, Otley 1895

Ridge Top, home of Emma Beecroft.

the Old Cloth Hall about 1 o'clock where Mr Gladstone had to address a mass meeting at 2. The assembly was immense, probably 30,000. Many had to be carried outside. Mr Gladstone arrived soon after 2. I had a good position for which I have paid five shillings, and I could hear every word. He is undoubtedly the finest orator I ever heard. Mrs Gladstone and their son Herbert, who is M.P. for Leeds, were also present. Herbert is a very promising young man. I staied in Leeds and attended a music hall and was much amused. Took train at 11. A most beautiful moonlight night. Walked all the way home from Otley. Arrived about 2 a.m. thoroughly tired.

Nowadays it is hard to believe that any countryman would rise at dawn, walk fourteen miles and pay five shillings (the equivalent perhaps of £5 or more today) to hear any politician.

Thursday, October 13. There is talk about the deficient water supply and drainage of the village, and it is thought that the sanitary authority will take the matter in hand and compel the proprietors [of houses?] to alter things. But the proprietors fear the cost and so we drink water highly polluted with sewage and our sinks are simply beastly. So much for the intelligent and industrious population who would suffer fevers and murrains sooner than spend a few pounds on purifying the water and improving the drainage.

Yes, the sanitary authority had to do it in 1884, at a cost of £350 which they recovered by rating the villagers.

Friday, October 14. Off to Otley by 9 o'clock. A very wild wet morning, in fact about the strongest wind with the heaviest rain that I ever remember seeing. I walked and having some good leather leggings and a top coat I got there without much hurt. The water was out at Otley bridge and I had to get carted over with a friend. This is the third time the river has been out this year. Got plenty to drink at Otley, that is whisky to keep out the cold. A pretty girl with whom I am half in love smiled very sweetly as she passed me on the way home which made my heart flutter. Got home about dusk.

Saturday, October 15. Very dry windy day. At home all day doing nothing much. Great disasters all over the country in consequence of the late storm. A hen drinking should have come off at the Inn tonight but it somehow missed. These hen drinkings originate as follows: when a wedding takes place some neighbouring young fellow waits upon the bridegroom and asks for the hen. The newly-wedded person usually gives the Hen in the shape of five shillings which is drunk at the village inn when all the young fellows meet and subscribe something to it and generally a roaring time is had of it. These things, like many other old customs, are not as popular as they used to be. Playing cards at Uncle George's till 11 o'clock.

Thursday, October 20. Milked and fettled cows then over to work at Beecrofts. Home to a very good dinner of lamb pie and followed by apple pie. Brother Charles arrived while we were at dinner to buy a calving cow. Jobbing about then and writing for the newspaper. I find it hard work studying composition but by dint of very close and laborious attention I can manage to produce a very creditable article on passing events.

Thursday, October 27. Up by 7, milked and got ready and off to Knaresborough with Jonathan Spence. Rode in his trap. Our business was to get sworn to serve on the jury, which is an ancient custom of the old Forest Court. All the townships in the Forest send representatives, most of them four men each.

The formality used at the Court is rather ludicrous and is looked upon as a matter more to laugh at than anything else. However the Court still serves some good in the matter of encroachments and the business brought before it does fully justify its continuance as a medium of justice in the ancient Forest of Knaresborough. Got a good dinner at the Boars Head. David Petty rode back with us. Called at Kettlesing Head, loosed out our horse and corned him. Got sundry ales and rather lively on getting home.

> *When the Forest of Knaresborough was formed in 1177 the inhabitants became copyhold tenants under the lord of the honour. The Court for the Forest was called the Sheriff Torne, or Great Court Leet. It was held in Knaresborough Castle twice a year, within a month after Easter and at Michaelmas. The Adjorned Court, called 'The Great Inquest' was held in different parts of the Forest. Principal business in 1881 was receiving surrenders, admitting copyhold tenants, presenting nuisances, receiving rents and fines for encroachments. The officers were a high steward, a learned steward, an under-steward, a bailiff, a grave (court crier) and Beadle, the last three chosen annually by the jury.*

Monday, November 7. Went round with Chas. Hemsley collecting (Prudential) insurance money. Went first to Blubberhouses, then to Fewston and afterwards to Norwood. I am taking over the agency and Hemsley is giving it up. It may bring about two shillings a week which helps just a little to meet payments.

Saturday, November 12. My birthday. I am 37 years old. Am getting on to be a young man yet. Weighed myself. 10 stones 3 lbs. I am slight, rather smart looking and pretty lish and active, but latterly I have felt symptoms of failing strength and action. Soon I shall go down the hill I expect.

Friday, November 25. Off to Otley by 8.30. Standing in market with sparerib and pork leaves . . . After getting my business done and it being the Latter Statutes, I went in for the usual follies, a glass here and there, a chat and a flirt with this girl and that, a crack at the shooting gallery . . . Visited the Japanese Bazaar at the Mechanics Institute in company with my cousin Fanny Procter and Clara Dickinson. Afterwards boozing about till 11 p.m. when I along with cousin Wm. Dickinson and Dick Holmes started on our dreary journey homeward. I arrived about 1.30 a.m. disgusted and tired.

Thursday, December 8. Down at White Crag at Aunt Mary's pig feast. Uncle George and Aunt Betsy and their girl Eliza, myself and mother and our little Georgy my nephew. We had a good supper of sparerib with a game of cards and plenty of whisky afterwards. Staied till 1 a.m. then home on a beautiful moonlight night.

Friday, December 9. Bought half an ounce of tobacco and two cigars. Purposes learning to smoke. Never fairly mastered it yet. At Otley. Pleasant walking there as it has frozen rather hard. Attended before Sanitary Committee about our village water supply. Home before dark having spent a very moderate and temperate day.

Tuesday, December 20. Snow commenced falling heavily. Very comfortable in the house. Smoking several pipes of tobacco. I don't think I am any worse in health for smoking although it makes me spit a good deal. But I am not yet master of it. I think of trying to master the habit and becoming a regular user of the weed as the habit of smoking seems to make one feel more sociable and contented.

Saturday, December 24. In Otley selling sparerib (yesterday) and taking drops of liquor. Market more busy on account of approach of Christmas. Hares sold at 6*s* 6*d* each. (Today) attended Robert Newsoms funeral. He died at Clint where he removed about half a year ago with his nephew and niece Mr and Mrs Kent. They had him brought to his old home at Snowden and took the coffin out of the hearse. It had a glass over the face. We had a good tea with ham at the house and a first-rate meat dinner at the Black Horse Inn at Askwith after the funeral. He was buried at Weston. So ends the Newsom family, Robert being the last left of the name. Home by dusk.

Sunday, December 25. Christmas Day. The boys shouting as usual. Gave them about three shillings. Wild and wet. Nothing at all going off. Staied at home all day. No place of worship.

Saturday, December 31. Up by 8. Milked then went to Norwood. Called at Chas. Holmes. Had cheese and gin. Also refreshed myself at John Patricks at Jack Hill as well as at Mr Friths. Registered a birth at James Dibbs and had some cleat wine with cheese. Registered a birth at John Taylors of Scow Hill. Also had tea and whisky. Came home. Attended Club meeting as secretary. Got a few more glasses of gin and staied till 11 o'clock. So it appears pretty plain that I finished the year 1881 carrying out the maxim laid down by Solomon, viz. eating and drinking and making merry.

The diarist's Biblical knowledge is a bit astray here, for the only scriptural counsel to eat, drink and be merry is in Ecclesiastes in the Old Testament and in St Luke's Gospel in the New.

The past twelve months have been fraught with no very important event for good or evil . . . I have continued the same frivolous weak-minded policy with regard to women, which has been so conspicuously my failing point in times past and the year 1881 finds me busy flirting with silly young girls and apparently as far off getting a wife as I was a year ago. At the commencement of last year I laid down a certain line of conduct which I hoped I might be able to carry out during the coming year. I regret to say that for the most part the reforms I then proposed have not been carried out . . . I have on various and frequent occasions taken more beer and spirits than was necessary or good for me . . . Then again I have been much remiss in the matter of industry. I have lacked that settled purpose in life and that feeling of hopefulness which is so essential in making headway in the world . . . I have been seriously wanting in moral and spiritual improvement. Instead of attending regularly at church or chapel on Sunday I have spent the day in idle gossip . . . I have saved about £50 which I suppose is not bad for a small affair in bad times.

1884

John Dickinson did not write the record for 1882 so that whether or not his pious intentions at the end of 1881 were carried out is unknown. He resumed entries in his diaries in 1884 with the usual preamble . . .

The year begins with open weather. Outdoor work progresses without interruption by frost or snow. Life in these country villages is quieter each year and the population gradually falls off so there is not that evidence of animation and hope in life which is found where the population is more numerous and young folk more plentiful. Altogether it is a dull routine . . . no games or amusements and no society to improve the culture or raise the intellect of the people. So we drift into the New Year.

Tuesday, January 1. Evening at Sunday School tea party at our village chapel. Many scholars said dialogues and pieces which they did very good indeed.

Saturday, January 19. Stripping Newsomes old mill at High Snowden. It now belongs to Captain Dawson of Weston Hall. Alas what havoc time does make. Not more than 50 years ago the mill rattled a cheerful merry tune and made good oatmeal. Now it is a ruin and the Newsome family who owned five farms and were a lusty race have fallen one after another by the fell hand of time and not one is left who bears the name . . . We all too will follow.

All's well that ends well
So says our greatest bard
But what is well we cannot tell
It all seems rather hard

Saturday, February 16. Collecting balance of insurance from parties at Fewston and Timble. I am giving up the job and be glad when I get out of it. A day of sorrow and disappointment. I feel as if my day had passed over and all is dark and gloomy.

Monday, March 3. Off to Pool by 8. Pleasant walk. Registered six births and deaths. Altogether a good day. Made 6*s* 6*d* fees.

Monday, March 24. A fine sunny day. At a place in the afternoon and submitted a question of importance. At Chas. Holmes then and had tea there. Then home and in evening attended meeting of committee for re-seating Fewston Parish Church.

> *There is no subsequent reference either to the 'place' or the important question — no hint that he had become a rejected suitor.*

> I am leading a sort of a gentleman's life
> And can do it so long as I haven't a wife
> But if I should take a fair maiden to kirk
> I very much fear I would then have to work

Tuesday, March 25. Writing out estimate for work at Snowden and met Cunliffe's agent who paid me a cheque for £31 for work done at Swinsty. Evening at annual ratepayers meeting and was reappointed waywarden. Staied till 12 o'clock drinking with a few friends.

Friday, March 28. Very dry pleasant walk to Otley and a good day throughout. Got paid for part bacon and manure. Also got orders for two flitches, 21 hundredweights of manure and took a good contract for masons work of Captain Dawsons agent, and sold 50 yards of waterworks hay. May I be sober and energetic and merit this blessing of Providence. Teetotal today and feels better in my head tonight.

Wednesday, April 19. Most beautiful weather. At High Snowden in forenoon jobbing about land. Grass is becoming plentiful and we shall soon have enough to turn the cattle out to. Meeting of the four by-law men of the Forest Court to look at water (supply) for Mrs Atkinson. Afterwards they all got drunk.

Good Friday, April 11. Up by 8 then went to Rhodes Renton for some mutton. Cuddled Patty, then at home jobbing about the house. Had another little episode with another girl. O John when will you learn wisdom? How silly, and I may say how wicked of you to give way to take advantage of poor innocent girls in that way. You rue afterwards as you do now. But what of that? You fall into the old habit again in a day or two. Your heart is very susceptible for your age. You are nearly 40 yet you are bothering with girls in their early teens. For shame, John. Look out for a young widow or a young old maid and don't bother no more after those bright young eyes which cannot be much good to you no way . . . Attended meeting of re-seating church committee in the evening.

Sunday, April 27. Home all day. Rather in a sulky mood. At no place of worship. I suppose it will please the Devil but I will give him the slip at the last.

Saturday, May 24. Working at William Beecrofts garden wall till noon then dressed up and had a walk in the evening and had a rolic with a young woman.

Sunday, June 29. Got up by 10 refreshed with a long night's rest. In the afternoon cousin William and I went fishing into Timble ghyll and got about 5lbs of trout. How sinful! But we do these bad and wicked things unthinking very often. May God forgive us.

Tuesday, August 12. Fixed letter-box for the Post authorities. First that has been placed at Timble. Sold a cow for £24 10*s*.

> Busy with a lot of little things
> My bow is strung with more than twenty strings
> Maidens young and old I cuddle and kiss
> All that comes to my net I reckon to be bliss
> But now I purpose to begin a better life
> And first of all I guess I'll get a wife

Thursday, August 28. Down at Swinsty Hall in the evening and arranged to lend Mr Bramley £150 at £7 (interest) per year.

Monday, September 8. Superintending taking down of old oak pews in Fewston Church. Timothy Patrick with three men doing the work, David Petty assisting. Came on wet towards night. Got a good feed of mushrooms to tea which I liked very much.

Wednesday, October 29. Wet wild forenoon. Went with Mr Wilks round by Peel Park and in afternoon saw the American Midgets. The man is 25 inches high and weighs 9 pounds. His wife is a little less and weighs 7 pounds. They were quite interesting. Took 4.30 train to Otley and thence home on foot.

Sunday, November 23. Up by 8 and attended cattle. Then went up to William Wilsons of Gill Beck to see John Wilson who has injured his fingers through a trap with a stone. It is my duty to visit him as Guardian in our sick club. The place is hemmed in by the bleak moors but is cosy and comfortable. A good peat fire and plenty of juvenile life about. A walk in the evening to Fewston. Keen frosty air and a bit of moon but a bright firmament of stars and a virtuous maiden into the bargain.

Monday, December 1. All covered with snow several inches deep. Busy first clearing gates and about the cattle. A somewhat grave event with a certain person which I fear cannot be of any good to me. I should have known better but I am so weak . . . Nothing very weighty but it veers toward a state of things that might develop to very scandalous and troublesome things for which I should be chiefly blameable. Got a new lamp which has a double burner and makes a capital light.

Saturday, December 6. Busy finishing off watering trough in fold. Evening at Uncle George's playing cards. Won 4*s* 1*d*. I don't care much for the game but it affords a little diversion from the dull routine of our village life. A good light a good fire and newspapers in the evening at home . . . In good health and fair hopes. Amongst other good and bad things I look forward to getting a wife some time within the next twenty years at farthest.

Thursday, Christmas Day. Up by 8. Several boys shouting their cheery salute before I got up. Keen frost and cold north wind, but fine and dry. Cuddled a girl in forenoon. Party of singers about. James Lister at the Inn very bad in convulsions and reported likely to die.

Wednesday, December 31. In bed all day feeling very poorly. Thus the year ends in pain and gloom. Friends are kind and make inquiries. Financially I have met with reasonable success, and on making up my accounts and taking stock I consider myself worth not less than £1,000. This I think may be considered a good figure for one who started with nothing. Besides I reckon I have lost about £200 in unfortunate and rotten speculation.

1889

Five years elapse before Dickinson resumes his diary. In the intervening time his mother has died and he employs a housekeeper. But the pattern of his life alters very little.

Tuesday, January 1. Busy writing most of today in connection with the end of the registration quarter. In the evening attended a party given by Miss Procter to her scholars which was attended by a good many grown-up young persons. Dancing music and other amusements followed and we held it out up to the small hours.

Friday, January 11. Off to Otley and saw my landlord, James Whitaker and we arranged for me to put up a stable and shed for a trap, and so if all goes well I shall have a horse and trap if not a wife during this year.

Monday, January 14. Very open mild weather. In moderate health. I weigh 10 stones within one pound. Never weighed any more for past few years. I am only slender man, but light-boned and pretty smart and wiry. I am a passable sort of man and used to be pretty strong for my weight . . . Got four fat pigs and busy cutting up and salting. We have got a great quantity of bacon and must try to make a sale soon if we can.

Sunday, January 27. Up by 8. Breakfast then walk down croft and right up to High Snowden road and on by Four Lane Ends. Good dinner of roast sparerib. Evening at Fewston Church. Company of cousin Fanny Procter both ways. Fanny a little jealous of another girl but made up after.

Monday, February 4. Very indolent, only writing a letter and calling about. At Aunt Mary's in the evening. Rural life is used up and what spirit there is left in old England concentrates in the great towns where all that is best in everything gradually centres.

Sunday, March 3. Forenoon at Uncle George's and in house.

Evening at church. Walked up with cousin Fanny. We seem to be engaged.

Wednesday March 6. Off to Pool by 8. Walked by Folly Hall, Norwood Bottom reservoir edge and through Leathley. Murky cold day. Evening practising music with Fanny.

Sunday, March 17. Attended love feast at our chapel. About 30 came from Otley and Clifton. Perhaps 40 spoke of their experiences. A good deal of it looks weak but we hardly know what is best to do. I have no faith in this excitement, but its effect is better than other sorts of excitement and we cannot ignore religious influences.

> *Religious fervour that followed John Wesley's preaching tours in the North was so strong that fourteen years after his death in 1791 a so-called 'love feast' in Bradford attracted crowds that stretched outside the old Octagonal Chapel in Great Horton like theatre queues far into the night. A local historian wrote that the doors were scarcely ever closed day or night for ten or twelve weeks, while people flocked to confess and convert — or as John Harland, a Bradford woolcomber and diarist put it, 'left the ranks of Satan and went over to the side of Emmanuel'.*

Sunday, March 31. A fine dry day and I walked round the land in the forenoon. Had the preacher Lockwood of Otley to tea. Mission band at night at the service. Walked with Fanny after. All very nice and sweet but withal exceedingly virtuous. Fanny is by far the most virtuous girl I ever came in contact with.

Tuesday, April 2. Up at 7. Good breakfast of boiled bacon and tea and bread . . . evening at public house. Had three bottles of ale with Charles Dibb and Samuel Demain, who set sail for America tomorrow. They were both drunk and will have to alter their conduct if they are to do any good in America.

Tuesday, April 9. In evening dressed up and had musical evening with cousin Fanny. Walked on with her after. She says we will be married soon, but the event gets put off from time to time so that I almost begin to doubt if it will come off at all.

Sunday, April 21. Evening at chapel. Mission from Friends here. George Holmes and his wife got converted. I somehow don't feel as if I could consistently begin openly professing religion. I am so full of unbelief. I trust that God in his mercy will remove these hindrances.

Saturday, May 11. Got ready and went to Otley. My real object was to accompany my cousin home. Went into show field but never saw such a quagmire. Walked home with Fanny from 8 to 10 o'clock. Pleasant journey. At Aunt Mary's till 11.

Sunday, May 19. Home until evening then at Fewston church. Most folks off to Brown Bank where very great doings are going off in the way of a revival. Evangelists with travelling van holding forth nightly.

Friday, May 31. Went to Fewston Chapel to hear Mr and Miss Bradford who are visiting places with a mission car. Extraordinary proceedings up to one o'clock in the morning. Several converts. It may be all for the good but the way of carrying it through looks very different from the reverent manner we usually associate with religious exercises.

Tuesday, June 11. Club walk at Timble. Tea party at chapel. I suppose hardly ever a more lively day was seen at Timble. About 100 members of the village lodge started in procession to Fewston Church headed by Otley Engineers Band of Musick, a good band. The day was most beautifully fine. The Lodge flag was carried in showy style and all passed off brilliantly. At the chapel close on 200 took tea. The Otley Mission Band was in force, about 30 of them, and made things lively. Kissing rings and other games occupied the young folk in the evening, and dancing at the Inn up to midnight. Altogether a high day for our poor old dull village, but I was miserable all day with indigestion.

Sunday, June 16. Today most beautiful. Walked to Four Lane Ends in forenoon and in evening at church. Walked with cousin Fanny after. Very sweet and pleasant. Fanny is a jewel of virtue surpassing all I have ever met with.

Sunday, June 23. Drought now getting rather severe. Good dinner of Yorkshire pudding and roast beef and new potatoes. Shaved and washed and dressed. Had preacher to tea. Evening at Church. Walked round by Three Lane Ends. Cousin Fanny on the road. Met her after and had just one kiss and nothing more.

Wednesday, June 26. Finished haytime about 4 o'clock. Got it all without a drop of rain. Abraham Moon and Mrs Moon arrived soon after noon in a carriage and staied two or three hours. They had dinner here. Went to Aunt Mary's in evening.

> The heat and work is very oppressive
> And my housekeeper is aggressive
> And grumbles much and makes a rout
> At me for going and staying out
> On nights so that she cannot sleep
> It makes her almost fit to weep
> Because she thinks I'm courting strong
> And may get married before long

Friday, July 5. Off to Otley by 8. Sent calving heifer over that we have bred. A beautiful little animal and quiet as a lamb. It almost makes me sad to part with the poor dumb uncomplaining creature. I am too tender-hearted to have commerce among cattle. I cannot bear to see them knocked about.

> Its sometimes up and sometimes down
> Until Death claims us as his own
> They say its either worse or better
> I don't believe its any hotter

Friday, July 19. Off to Otley by 8 to meet Mr Newstead to examine my copies of registration. Busy for a couple of hours and then took 2.23 train to Leeds in company with cousin Fanny. Bought wedding ring and gold watch and albert for Fanny. Price of ring £1 8*s*, watch £7 10*s*, albert £2 15*s*. Seems rather a heavy payment. Total paid £11, but as I love Fanny I did it cheerfully. It seems as if we should be married before long unless unforeseen events happen.

Saturday, July 27. Forenoon round paying men at Chas. Holmeses, Joseph Gills and Henry Bramleys. Robinson Gill here a few hours. Presented me with a set of American current coins, over £4 in value. He is a very generous man in every sense.

Wednesday, August 7. Sold twelve hams and two flitches, hams at 9½*d.* per lb and flitches 7½*d.* Took train up to Ilkley. Saw the vicar and got licence to get married, or rather, paid for it as it has to come by post in a few days. Paid £2 6*s*. which looks dear, but we do such foolish things. Train back to Otley. Walked home.

Saturday, August 10. Had letter from Robinson Gill who is in Paris at present. Also got marriage licence by post today.

Monday, August 12. Working hard and fast all day at Chas. Holmes barn. In evening dressed up smart and down to Fewston Chapel tea party. Came up with Fanny. She promised to marry me in about a month, so if nothing intervenes I am likely to get wed at last and how folk will talk. I am so well known and such an old bachelor [he is 45], but I suppose it will get over like all other events.

Thursday, August 15. Robinson Gill came a little before noon and had talk on question of him building and endowing a reading room for Timble. In evening Mr Gill and I with Willy Kendall and Uncle George sat down to supper at village inn. A brace of moor game were provided, the first I ever tasted, and all at Mr Gill's cost. He sails on Saturday.

Sunday, August 25. Talk with Fanny about visit to Paris and getting married.

Monday, August 26. Wrote off to Cooks agency for tickets for Paris. Evening at public house and got three whiskys.

Monday, September 9. At home all day getting little matters ready for wedding. The event naturally causes me to feel somewhat reflective, but upon the whole I am hopeful and feels that it is the right thing to do as it is the way that the silent voice of Providence directs. All seems favourable so far.

Tuesday, September 10. Up by 6.30. Most beautiful fine morning. All bustle getting ready for the important event. Got dressed in good time. Cab arrived before 10. Got in and on to Fanny's place and we drove down to Fewston. Brother Charles and wife, Peter Patrick and wife, Henry Procter and girl from Otley. Also Mrs Ellen Thackwray all went down with us. A good many others turned up and all passed off very well. Staied a little at public house, then up to breakfast, after which drove off to Otley to take the 2.33 train to Leeds and the 3.40 train to London. Staied all night at Ye Old Bell Hotel near St. Paul's Cathedral. Very warm and close and well tired with the excitement and bustle.

Wednesday, September 11. Not very well. Appetite bad. Visited

St. Paul's Cathedral. Up in Whispering Gallery. After that a ride in steamboat from Blackfriars Bridge to Chelsea. Ride back through City to Bank, then to lodgings. Took 7.10 train at Holborn Viaduct for Dover. Then steamboat to Calais. Arrived there about midnight. Strange scenes and language. Waited over an hour at Calais. Got off at last and had about a six or seven hours ride before getting to Paris. The trains don't go near so fast as our English ones do. Cooks had conveyance waiting and we drove to Hotel Rapp. Very tired indeed on getting there.

Fewston Church.

Thursday, September 12. Neither myself nor Fanny felt able for much work today so we only looked round a little and went to bed early. I was very unwell on account of appetite being bad. Very hot weather. Very sweet rest and loving fellowship with my dear wife. Parisian life is very novel and charming.

Friday, September 13. Up by 8. Most beautiful weather. One of Cooks conveyances holding 36 passengers started off at 9 o'clock for Versailles and St. Cloud. We had pleasant company and quite a jolly day. The drive through the avenues and boulevards was delightful. Indeed the beauty of the scene all along the route was something wonderfully beautiful. Saw the ruined palace at St. Cloud, then on to Versailles and saw the wonderful palace and fine avenues. To the hotel by 6 and dinner of eight courses which was somewhat tedious. Had a good interpreter with our party.

Saturday, September 14. Drive with Cooks party through Paris and saw Column Vendome, Rue de Rivoli, Tuileries, Louvre and various places of interest. Hotel to dinner. Walk in city after. All very lively.

Sunday, September 15. Up by 7.30. After breakfast attended Mass at the Madeleine. Most beautiful church, but sad mummery carried on in the service. About hotel till dinner, then in Exhibition. Attended a variety concert. All wonderful lively. Sunday seems to be their day for pleasure-taking. Changed to Hotel Nice & Florence.

Monday, September 16. Up at 7.30. To Hotel Rapp for breakfast, then to Exhibition. Ascended to second floor of the Eiffel Tower. Regretted not going to the top. Wonderful view of Paris. Dinner by 4, then took conveyance to Nord station and 6.10 train to Calais where we arrived about 12.

Tuesday, September 17. Stepped on boat about 1 o'clock and crossed in two hours or rather under. Then train to London. Arrived about 6. Cab to Old Bell and to bed for about five hours.

Wednesday, September 18. Forenoon at Tower of London. Afternoon at Crystal Palace, a very wonderful place. London is a very wonderful city and the traffic in the streets is wonderful to look at.

Thursday, September 19. Up at 7. By Underground Railway to Westminster. Visited the Abbey. Venerable pile. Also the Horse Guards. Back to hotel and then 12.20 train to Leeds. Staied in Leeds till 8.10 train to Otley. Had telegraphed to Otley for a conveyance and a cab was waiting at the station, so we drove off in aristocratic style. Arrived home about 10.30, very tired — but married.

Tuesday, September 24. Not quite recovered from effects of honeymoon with the consequent excitement and toil. Spent all day in house writing. Fanny does first rate and we get along very sweetly so far.

Wednesday, September 25. All day at Chas. Holmeses barn flagging it. My wife working away at her new duties cheerfully and efficiently.

Sunday, October 6. Forenoon in house. Fanny made capital rabbit pie to dinner. Chapel in afternoon, church in the evening.

Monday, November 4. Working all day at Beecrofts at Ridge Top building new cartshed and walling gap at waterworks. Fanny washing and all quite happy and domestic like. Very happy with Fanny who works well and keeps all clean and is rather a clever housekeeper so I think.

Saturday, November 16. John Bramley of East End, died today, the wealthiest man in our parish.

Saturday, December 7. Self and wife attended entertainment at Board School, Fewston, given by the master, Mr Whitaker and scholars. Large attendance. Beautiful frosty moonlight night. Bought seven fat pigs off Joseph Thackwray of Sourby.

Friday, December 13. At Otley. Also Fanny. We walked both ways. Expended about £5 in cutlery and pots. Home by 6 . . . Fanny is a good sweet pure woman and suits me well.

Monday, December 23. Wet day. Jobbing about a bit. Helping Fanny twining mangle which is very pleasant for a newly-married man.

Wednesday, Christmas Day. Usual shouting of boys before daylight. Day quiet enough. Nothing going off in village anyway. Fanny and I dined at her mothers.

Saturday, December 28. Had Frank Gill (from America) to supper, also Andrew Dickinson, Joseph Holmes and Aunt Mary with a few others. Roast goose and sparerib. Parlour and other places well lighted and all looked cheerful and comfortable. Held till about 12 o'clock, drinking whisky and talking.

The past year has had, as usual for me, days of joy and days of sorrow, though perhaps upon the whole brighter days than in most of the years gone by. In addition to a fair amount of business prosperity it has consisted of days of courtship and days of married life. The days of courtship lasted up to the tenth of September when I took Fanny to Fewston Church and we were united in wedlock. Though not possessing wealth to feel quite independent we have sufficient which, if used with judicious care, and keeping an eye on the main chance, we can live easily without having to do the harder sort of labour which most people are under the necessity of performing. I purpose keeping a horse next year and hopes to get assistance in getting about the country thereby.

1891

I again begin keeping a diary after giving it up during the year 1890. During the past year I have enjoyed the sweets and bitters of matrimony and I don't find much fault with married life. It curtails a good deal of that freedom in social intercourse so dear to bachelors but it puts in its place many joys and comforts to which a bachelors life is a stranger. It may be that I have been more than usually fortunate in getting the wife I have. I am not going to say that she is without faults, but I will say that she possesses some very good qualities. She is of very cleanly habits and has improved the appearance of our house, although it was not badly managed before. Her virtue and truthfulness I believe to be unimpeachable. Of course she has got a little bit of temper — what woman of any worth is without? — but I am compelled to say that any little tiffs we may have had during the past year have been mainly due to shortcomings on my part. I have been used to command and to be obeyed at home, and go in and out at my own pleasure without anyone daring to interfere. If my wife has sometimes grumbled a bit and a few sharp words have passed, if has purified the air. Thus the year has passed over fairly prosperous.

Thursday, January 1. Most of December has been a time of frost and snow, and the severe weather continues. Today I got two fat pigs from West End and cut up and salted them. Cousin Andrew Dickinson is in partnership with me in the salting business. Last year we netted about £22 out of it.

Friday, January 2. Off to Otley by 8.30. I drive in my own conveyance now. My cousin Eliza Dickinson, aged 19, rode with me, a big stout fine-looking girl, but I fear lacking the moral grit so essential in female character.

Thursday, January 22. Gets up now from 8 to 9 every day all along. Wild snow showers in forenoon. George, my nephew, yoked up horse and cart and went to Otley for some coals. Got seven hundredweight at one shilling per cwt. Hung bacon and did other little duties. Am very nicely off all along.

Friday, January 23. Ice and snow on the ground. Started for Otley at 10. Joe Holmes rode with me. Very miserable weather and few people in Otley. Took in my plan of districts for the census to Mr Newstead, and attended Highway Board meeting. Started home about 3.30 in a very heavy downfall of rain which continued all the way to Timble.

Monday, January 26. Went to look at Worsal Crag quarry with a view to opening a place for felling stones. David Petty joined me at Fewston. Went round by the inn. Got a few glasses too many I fear. Home by seven somewhat worse for inebriating liquors. Wife a bit cross and myself silent, so the evening passed over and to bed in due course.

Tuesday, January 27. Evening about library work, fixing arch to library porch.

Monday, February 2. Meeting of library trustees. Talk about buying Wood Farm as suggested by recent letter from Mr (Robinson) Gill. Masons fixed west chimney on Robinson library.

Sunday, February 8. Chapel in evening. Metcalfe of West End the preacher. He storms out something extraordinary for loudness.

Thursday, February 12. To Folly Hall, thence to Jack Hill and Fewston where George had taken horse to get shoes fastened. Then took horse and saddle on to Menwith Hill. We have men working at all these places. Mr Marshall, architect from Otley here and I spent an hour with him. Sold him piece of old oak furniture for ten shillings which I bought at Michael Woods sale for one shilling, so that is good profit.

Sunday, March 1. Forenoon in house reading Thackray's *Vanity Fair.* Fanny off teaching Sunday School. Fanny is a little given to good things that way.

Wednesday, March 18. Called at Crag House, Norwood Top yesterday and registered illegitimate birth for Maria Rathmell. So sorrows come to poor girls. Drove on home in cold north wind. Sarah Hudson buried today. A person of unfortunate reputation, 41 years old. Seduced by her stepfather at 15, and had several children by him since. Who shall say how much allowance ought to be made for the errors which society condemns in her case?

Friday, March 20. Mr James Berry of Bradford, the public hangman, came with Frank Dickinson to Timble with view to buying our hams . . . In evening he was at the village inn. Of course his visit caused a little excitement. He is a jolly sociable figure, medium size, fresh looking, with quick piercing eyes and some histrionic abilities. Can tell a story with good effect and looks anything but a typical hangman when in social intercourse. He seems to take a drop too much at times, but is pretty wide awake as to No. 1.

Saturday, April 4. Saddled horse and visited every house in the township of Blubberhouses delivering schedules for the census. Then walling bricks at library. Joiners laid oak floor of entrance hall. Census work being upon us I am somewhat occupied with that, and hopes to clear about £6 out of it.

Tuesday, April 7. Making up enumeration book for census. Wife throng with making hearthrug, Alice Spence helping her.

Saturday, May 2. Much influenza about and the people sorely oppressed. Several deaths have occurred. Many families are in a poor way all being ill and nobody to look after them. My wife all night with her mother who is very ill of it . . . I drink a lot of whisky which I think helps to ward off influenza.

Thursday, May 7. Wife staying all night with her mother who is very weak . . . Thomas Rickard, a labourer for the waterworks died yesterday from influenza. William Wilson of Gill Becks, Blubberhouses, is also dead from the same cause. I registered deaths of the Scotts of Norwood, mother and daughter.

Saturday, May 16. Very cold north wind. Got up at 2 a.m. and found cow had calved. George got up also and we did the necessary things and George went back to bed but I sat up remainder of the night. It got colder and colder and snow fell. My wife has been unwell lately but is getting better. She is in what is sometimes described as an interesting condition.

Wednesday, May 20. In afternoon Fanny and I drove over to look at her place at Kettlesing. It is a small farm of about 12 acres. She and her brother Henry are joint owners of it. Had tea with Mrs Wilson and came home. Very cold north wind prevails.

Friday, May 29. At Otley. Drove. Sister rode there with me. Got fit on for two new teeth, bottom front ones. All the rest of my teeth are fairly sound and good so that I don't show amiss in that respect.

Sunday, June 7. At home all day. Uncle George came at 2 and sat till 10, eight hours without leaving the seat. What a time to sit. He is very big and heavy.

Saturday, June 20. Very hot and over-powering from early morning. Almost everybody off to sham fight of volunteers at Weston Hall. Quiet evening walk with Fanny to Timble Ghyll. Caught some fish and had them fried on getting home.

Wednesday, July 1. Visited Buffalo Bills Wild West. Yoked trap and Andrew Dickinson and I started about 9 and took train for Pool. Called there and registered three births, then by 1 o'clock train to Leeds and went on to Cardigan Field. Paid three shillings for seat to witness the performance of the cowboys, Indians, etc. Wonderful spectacle.

Wednesday, July 8. At dinner Fanny began to have pains and sent for her mother and Mrs Lister. George saddled the horse and fetched Dr Ritchie from Otley. The child was born just before he arrived, about 4 p.m. A girl. It is before its time they say and two months before we expected it. It is rather small.

Monday, July 13. Busy among the hay. Got about three parts out of four of Town Field into large cocks. Very nice hay but rather light crop. Dr Ritchie called to see wife and chiid just after noon.

Wednesday, July 15. Busy amongst hay. Got Town End about half of it carted and other half into cock. Rain came on then . . . Much startled to hear that Dr Ritchie died this morning about 8 o'clock.

Saturday, July 25. Finished hay-time today. Carted last load about 4 o'clock.

Tuesday, July 28. Up at 6.30 at school house in forenoon. Caught three fish in Timble Ghyll and gave them to two boys who had been fishing in Swinsty Reservoir but caught only one. Our infant is doing fairly well. Wife somewhat down this morning as her assistant, Alice Spence, was poorly and could not come. Got a nice few mushrooms. Cut up a ham today that was defective at the shank. Our hams are turning out very badly this season, most of them ailing more or less at the shank.

Monday, August 3. Timble Feast. Young fellows playing quoits. In the evening young people from around and pretty lively doings for a few hours. Young men and women playing kiss in the ring, elders drinking at the Inn. A batch singing dancing, others patronising the shooting gallery, Aunt Sallies, etc.

Wednesday, August 19. Registered birth of our little daughter. We call it Dorothy Mary. People laugh at the name Dorothy but I suppose custom will wear off the novelty . . . She sucks her mother's breasts and also gets nourishment out of a bottle and tube.

Wednesday, August 26. Very high wind and heavy rain in night. Large bough of tree blown off and in our front garden. In evening had two beers at village inn but am a bit disgusted with inn company. Those who are mostly found there are almost all on the downgrade, so I think I shall attend less.

> Some folk are careful all their time
> Through early youth and manhood's prime
> While others drink and rant about
> As years come in and years go out
> At last all die and pass away
> What follows after who can say?

Thursday, September 3. Evening down at Fewston and attended political meeting. The Unionist van 'Balfour' was there with two paid agents to advocate Conservative principles. Mr Wyvill, of Denton Hall, the Unionist candidate for the Otley division was there and gave an address. He is only an indifferent talker. I am well tired of political meetings at present. Up home by 11.

Tuesday, September 8. Charles Hobson from Bland Hill here in the evening for a death certificate for his brother Harry. Poor Harry. He was an idiot for years. His chief occupation was tending cattle on the highways and often caused amusement by striding a stick and imagining himself mounted on horseback at full gallop.

Thursday, September 12. Yoked our horse into brothers trap and brother and I with our wives drove to Harrogate. Left horse at Ship Inn and took the 11.26 train to Ripon, then hired a cab to take us to Studley and Fountains Abbey. Exceedingly warm day and somewhat overdone with it, but the out was pleasant. We drove to the Minster at Ripon and inspected the noble fabric. Then on through Market Square. It was market day, and forward to Studley. The walks at Fountains are very lovely and must have cost a lot to lay out. At last the Abbey burst upon our view, grand and impressive, filling us with wonder at the genius which brought out such wonderful design in such a dark age.

Tuesday, September 15. Up by 7. At Joseph Moons at Fewston. We are preparing for building a buttress to the front of his cowhouse. Joseph is all that is left of the Moons at Fewston and he clings to it after the buildings are likely to fall down. Formerly the Moons had the corn mill and were a family of first note in the then busy village of Fewston. Now the corn mill is swallowed by the waterworks, the trade has passed away, and Joseph, a bachelor of about 60, is all that is left of the family.

Wednesday, September 16. In forenoon assisted by nephews John and George Archer pointing and repairing our own buildings. After dinner saddled horse and rode over the moor to Denton. First called at Dunkirk Farm and then almost all the farm houses in Denton township gathering the rate. It was a very bothering in and out business but I got through and enjoyed the ride round. Returned by the High Gait over the moor which was a very long rough and dreary road but full of a grand silent impressiveness. Farming in Denton seems very dead and spiritless as indeed it is all over. I cannot help thinking that a great decadence has come over the farms and folk during my time. Revival services are being held just now every evening in our chapel. Much stir amongst those given that way. For myself I somehow am in doubt about all theology and must experience a great change of heart before I can have the needful faith to become a genuine Christian.

Saturday, October 3. Forenoon at Menwith Hill to pay workmen. The barn is almost ready for roofing. About ten men at work. It will cost Mr Bramley a lot of money. Just now there is much gossip current about a pending breach of promise against Mr Bramley by a Miss Newall. A foolish man he has been to bother in that quarter.

Thursday, October 8. In the evening I took a flitch to the Sun Inn, Norwood, also weighed and put in the cart 14 flitches and one ham ready to take to Ilkley and Otley tomorrow. We have now sold out of our bacon. We have had a greater amount of uncured than I ever knew us have before. This hurts the job a lot. We have lost by the insolvency of the Middleton Hotel in Ilkley. Still it will pay a little I think.

Monday, October 19. King Grange removed from Timble to Otley today. King has had a somewhat chequered career. Of illegitimate birth was in service in early years and had women and illegitimate children. Married and then his wife died and he married a widow. Daughter had a child by him. Then his second wife died and he lived on with daughter and sons. Daughter already grown into a nice young woman. But then the daughter died a year or two ago and latterly King and a soft lad lived at Timble. Very good neighbours with all their faults.

Saturday, October 24. The roof is now on Mr Bramleys barn ready for alting. A very superior building and the best barn that we have ever built. Evening club night and acted as secretary. The Lodge is again prosperous and worth about £1,015. Had a glass or two of whisky and a game or two of bagatelle.

Thursday, November 5. In the evening boys going round shouting

> Remember, remember its Fifth of November
> A stick and a stake for King George's sake
> If you don't gi' me a coal
> I'll bon a hole i' yer owd hedge boddam

And they mostly got the coal and later on had a bonfire and romping rough play followed till 11 p.m. or later.

Monday, November 9. Down at Swinsty Hall in evening, took proposal to insure buildings on all Mr Bramley's property. He talks of leaving Swinsty and going to live in Harrogate. He is much troubled on account of an action for breach of promise of marriage brought against him by a Miss Newall of Fewston. The man has made a complete fool of himself. So we all do at some time or other.

Saturday, November 14. Washed and dressed and good breakfast. Yoked trap and drove to Menwith to pay workers. Wages of the masons 8½*d* an hour.

Tuesday, December 1. Went to Swinsty Hall with insurance policy for Mr Bramley against fire for £1,400. He paid me £2-0-6*d* as premium. He is removing to Harrogate pending breach of promise action . . . but [it has been] settled by Mr Bramley paying her £200. So the rumour is crushed in the bud.

Saturday, December 12. Down at cousin Williams in forenoon. They had a child died named Stanley. Frost last night and snow on the ground . . . I have a lot of money laying in business now, £300 to £400. I think it is all in safe hands however.

Friday, December 25. Only six boys came Christmassing this morning, the fewest I remember. The day has been quiet as possible. There is no young life or spirit left in the old country. Our Dorothy is far from well. Fanny baking tarts for a tea party tomorrow.

Saturday, December 26. Informal opening of the Robinson Library. Busy putting up and trimming lamps, and got all lit up and ready for 3.30 p.m. West End choir gave service of song. Considering weather a good attendance. Rooms looked splendid. Music during tea, and all passed off beautifully.

Sunday, December 27. George looked into the Library about 9.30 and found that it was on fire under the hearth of the north-east fireplace. It had been smouldering all night and it is a miracle that the place was not burned down. We got it out by knocking the plaster off under the floor in the lower basement room. Dorothy much better.

1892

The year opens fair and well so far as I can see with regard to my family affairs and business prospects. I purpose by God's blessing to try to do my duty so far as I am able in face of the frailties to which I am subject. I purpose trying to overcome a spirit of indolence which has beset me a good deal lately, and beginning a more solid and sound business system with the New Year.

Friday, January 1. Beautiful morning with a slight frost. Pleasant drive to Otley and had rather a busy day doing many small errands. At Dr Malcolm's on vaccination, also at Dr Williamson's on the same business.

> *With his building business expanding he has taken his cousin William into partnership but it becomes an uneasy arrangement.*

Saturday, January 2. Drove to Menwith Hill and paid men. It has been a long and costly job (new barn for Mr Bramley) I think my partner, cousin Bill, does not know how to run a job to advantage. It is simply beggaration the system he has inaugurated of making such good work. The country cannot afford it. Back home at 2 through a boisterous wind. In evening made out accounts for Mr Bramley.

Wednesday, January 13. Down at Fewston to meet supervisor for licence for my trap, price 15 shillings. A good many farmers met at the Inn to get exemptions for dogs. I staied a few hours and had a few glasses of whisky and social talk.

Monday, January 18. Gets daily paper and keeps things going as to current news. Much talk just now about death of the Duke of Clarence, heir to the throne.

> *Clarence, Prince Albert Victor was the eldest son of Edward VII and Queen Alexandra. His death at the*

age of 28 led to his younger brother becoming George V in 1910.

Thursday, January 21. Got fat pig from Joseph Moon of Fewston. Life is very dull at Fewston to what it used to be. In fact all country places are comparatively dead to what they were 30 years ago. It is due to the rapid development of invention, and especially steam power which has annihilated distance and made it more convenient getting to the towns.

If country life is rather down
All is not pleasant in the town
When Spring comes round with life and song
What care we for the busy throng?
Where smoke and dirt o'erclouds the sky
And townsmen for the country sigh

Monday, January 25. Round by Swinsty Hall to see Mr Pennington about selling him some hay. Hay is looking up and our prospects mending that way. We have about 700 yards — by we I mean myself and cousin William — but all the money paid is mine. Letter from Robinson Gill in New York stating that he has decided to run a school along with the library at Timble.

Monday, February 1. Hung two pigs in forenoon. Very wild and wet and no outdoor work. Only poor profits so far this season.

Times are not so very good
Although I do not want for food
But money is not made so fast
As it has been back in the past
But I have hopes of better times
And then I'll write more hopeful rimes

Monday, February 8. David Petty drunk at the village inn. In consequence of a dispute we have with him in reference to some iron work supplied at Henry Bramleys villa he makes a point of insulting both Cousin Bill and me whenever we meet with him when he is drunk. Today he used most insulting language and in my temper — I was shovelling gravel — I threw a shovefull right on top of him. He was very frightened and calmed down. I don't like bother of this sort.

Wednesday, February 10. In afternoon attended sale at White Crag at Stephen Teals place. Distress sale, his tenant William Gibson. I bought bedding and bedstead for sixpence.

Monday, February 15. Evening in house reading. Takes *[Leeds] Mercury* daily, also *Otley Observer* weekly and gets sent *Bradford Observer Budget* weekly and *Tit-Bits* almost every week besides *Once a Week* from R. Gill in New York, so I am fairly off for reading matter.

Tuesday, February 16. Somewhat depressed. Feels that I am cut off from civilising influences through the decadence of village life. I think I should have made a much better man if I had gone out when young to where men are centralised and where the volume of life is bigger. But why regret? For of all sad words of tongue and pen the saddest are these: it might have been.

Thursday, February 18. Measuring hay in forenoon. We have five haystacks on the reservoir grounds having had hardly any sale for three years. I think there will be a great scarcity this season and we may sell a good deal of our old stock to advantage. Weighed bacon flitch for Richard Holmes, price 7½*d* per lb.

Wednesday, February 24. Snow and slush still covering roads. Simply doing nothing at all. Must stir up when the weather mends as I have a wife and child who are supposed to stimulate me to greater exertion.

> Our baby is a wondrous child
> So pure and sweet and undefiled
> Her smile is heaven, her eyes are gray
> And look just like the dawn of day

Tuesday, March 1. Excitement on account of election for County Council member. Colonel Dawson of Weston Hall and Thomas Horsman of Ilkley are the candidates. Mr Horsman was at our house today. He is not a man of very good appearance and not such a man as I would think likely to fill the position with credit or dignity therefore I shall vote for Dawson.

Thursday, March 3. Polling day. Voted at Board School for Colonel Dawson. All went for Dawson here, both Liberal and Conservative. Dawson got in by a majority of 482 votes.

The Colonel is of a jolly sort
His otter hounds afford good sport
His eloquence is not so fine
His power lies not in that line
Its acres and his purse that tell
And such as Horsman know it well
Although despotic days are past
Money will move us to the last

Friday, March 4. Very cold and still frosty. At Otley then on to Pool on ordinary business. Then back to Otley by 12.17 train. Snow covers the high hills.

O for a throstle's note so sweet
In place of frost and snow and sleet
Snowdrops are all that yet appear
To tell us of the changing year
Soon will the ides of March pass o'er
And Spring return as its done before
And ghylls and moors be loud with song
The flowers bloom as we pass along

Saturday, March 5. Got order from Joseph Moon to proceed with slating work at Jane Wigglesworth's of Cragg Hall. About 400 yards of stripping and slating is to do so I think we shall have a fairly good job. Mason prospects are very good and work plentiful.

Monday, March 7. Forenoon at Cousin Bill's. Poor Bill is quite down. His health is bad and his luck worse. He has lost about £70 the last two years in his farming business so that his hard-earned money at masons work has all gone to make out the loss . . . I trust and hope that he may soon have better health and better luck. I myself don't feel so confident of success as I used to be. The energy of youth has gone by and the hard work of 25 years of masonry has left its effects on my constitution although I am still fairly active. I don't think I could stand a hard days work.

Friday, March 11. Cutting snow first thing to open way to Otley, but so wild and winterly that I did not go but sent George with cart. Idling about at home all day.

Sunday, March 13. Cow calved in evening all right. A bull calf. Not a farmer myself but runs about seven acres for convenience.

Reading *Robert Elsmere* by Mrs Humphrey Ward, a book after my own opinions on religion.

Monday, March 14. Indolent but must rouse myself up to energy and industry. Dorothy is growing and another on the way, so who can tell the responsibilities which may follow?

Wednesday, March 16. Jasper and John at School House, Fewston, altering set pot flue. This job has been the most unsuccessful contract we ever had, having lost us about £15. I mostly attribute it to my partner being so anxious to make good work and to his failure to know how to run the workmen. He may learn better by and by, but Cousin William is poorly all along.

Friday, March 18. Off by 7 o'clock and drove right along to Arthington Hall to register birth for Mr Thorp. In addition to thc 3*s* 7*d* in fees I got a gratuity of five shillings which put me in good spirits.

Sunday, March 20. A very fine day. Walked to Timble Ghyll in forenoon, but no life as yet. All is still and dead as winter. At home with Dorothy in afternoon. Evening at Chapel love feast. Very crowded. Very many speakers. These are simple homely experiences told in plain homely language. They all seem happy in Christ. They certainly seem to possess something to which I am a stranger.

Thursday, March 24. Letting lanes eatage. Got three whiskys. Evening at towns meeting. Attended as waywarden and was again appointed to the office. We had about 31 shillings to expend. Nine of us sat down to supper of ham and eggs and tea, anything we chose to drink. Distribution of prizes also took place at Wesleyan Chapel and good talking going off.

Friday, March 25. Off to Otley by 8.30. Took 11 train to Leeds, Fanny along with me. Staied in Leeds till 5 p.m. Bought over £2 of things. Bought pair of spectacles, my first start in that line, price 14 shillings. Got them of Franks. Back to Otley by 5 o'clock train and home by 8. Well tired and much expended. I think we shall have to try to pull up our expenditure or it will exceed the income.

Monday, March 28. One inch of ice formed during the night, and very cold indeed. Mr Peel came about hay in afternoon . . . Sold seven yards at five shillings per yard. Then at stack assisting Peel to cut.

For four years past no hay was sold
Though winters were both long and cold
But change is here and now's my time
To sell hay dear and write bad rime

Wednesday, March 30. Running about after various work. I am full of various business, to wit, mason work, registrations of births and deaths, vaccinations, bacon curing, farming, paraffin selling, tea selling, waterworks superintendent, highways collector, manure agent, insurance agent, hay dealer, and I don't know what besides. Too many irons in the fire, I almost think.

Thursday, April 28. All white with snow. As I was very tired through rheumatic pains in house all forenoon writing. Afternoon at White Crag. We have about 18 men at work in various ways. Hopes I may have energy to look after them properly.

Life is real say what we may
So let us live from day to day
And do our duty well and true
So that our days we may not rue

Thursday, May 5. Evening at Cousin Bill's to meet J.M. Bramley who has just removed from Harrogate to The Grange at Norwood. J.M. is a bachelor with a devoted housekeeper.

Thursday, May 26. Working hard all day at White Crag walling. Don't like this hard work as it is dirty, but I can do it very well yet, though being out of practice makes one rather shy of it.

Tuesday, May 31. No sleep at all last night. Fanny took ill about midnight. Gradually got worse. Sent for doctor about one o'clock. Prematurely delivered of child about 2 o'clock . . . She was very much exhausted and we had a very anxious time. But she came round and got apparently out of danger. Took the infant down to Fewston for burial.

Wednesday, July 6. General election the main talk now. Yesterday's return less favourable to the Liberals. The contest centres on the Irish Home Rule question. It is a very difficult problem for our statesmen. Mr Gladstone is the leader of the Liberals and the Home Rule Party. The Conservatives and dissident Liberals are opposed to home rule. Much bitterness is prevalent.

Friday, July 8. Off to Otley by 9. Got sworn in as personating agent for the Liberal candidate. Mr Wyvill, the Conservative candidate addressed the electors from the White Horse balcony, a good many of the local gentry supporting him. Bought linoleum for house floor. Much expense all along but hopes to be making good profits.

In the election the Liberals had a majority of 40 in the country, ousting the Conservative Government of the Marquess of Salisbury. On 18 August Mr Gladstone became Prime Minister for his fourth and last term.

Friday, July 15. Off to Otley by 9. Mr Robinson Gill of New York there. Busy with him in Otley and he came home with me and staied all night at our house. I suppose he is the wealthiest man that would ever have slept in this house. I dare say he will be worth upwards of half a million sterling. He is well pleased with the library building.

Tuesday, July 26. Busy at library. £100 worth of books arrived by carrier from Leeds. Also oil painting of Mr Robinson Gill. Very much strained about getting things ready, but hopes to get through.

Tuesday, August 2. Opening of the Robinson Library and Free School. Very busy forenoon. The Rev. Robert Collyer, the eminent Unitarian Minister, came about noon and dined at our house.

Timble village hall, built by John Dickinson.

Carriages rolled in and by the time for commencing, 2 o'clock, a very lively scene presented itself. The large room was crowded. Mr Collyer's address was a noble and eloquent discourse worthy of any occasion however exalted. Mr Gill spoke well and all passed off brilliantly. In the evening a variety of entertainment was given. The place again crowded to excess. This has been a great day for Timble and it is to be hoped will lead on to good in many ways.

Friday, August 5. Yesterday drove Mr Gill round, first to Swinsty Hall where we had a look round the house of his ancestors. In the evening Mr Gill gave dinner to the Library trustees. Uncle George Dickinson also present. Very pleasant time and two bottles of wine drunk. Off to Otley today, a somewhat excited morning as Mr Gill was departing from our village once more to take ship for America, which he will do tomorrow at 4 o'clock. He seemed a bit upset but we got off at last. Mr Gill took train about 3. Parted with him near the church. Back home somewhat relieved of the strain which Mr Gill's visit has occasioned.

Monday, August 15. I am altogether out of sorts. I have no appetite and suffer from mental and physical depression so that just now life is almost a burden. I have much bothering business in hand. We have a lot of mason work to do.

Monday, August 29. In much better health and can eat anything almost. We have a very strong force of men on now (16 men working on alterations to Uncle George's home) and I am obliged to do what I can looking after them.

Sunday, September 11. At home in forenoon. Roast duck and peas to dinner. Bro. Chas. and his wife and Lillie Moon arrived to dinner. Drove to Fewston Church about 3 and got our Dorothy christened. A wettish day. Dorothy behaved splendidly.

Monday, October 17. Off to Otley by 8.30. Pleasant drive. Mrs Barnes our new school mistress joined me there and we went to Leeds by the 11 o'clock train. Bought about £20 worth of apparatus for the school at Arnolds in Briggate. Newspapers full of accounts of destructive floods in Yorkshire.

Monday, October 24. The Robinson Library School began today and there were present 16 scholars.

Monday, October 31. Busy getting ready for opening Reading Room this evening. A pretty good muster of villagers drew up and evening spent in music. I don't know how the affair will go. The population is so small and intellectual pursuits are unpopular.

Tuesday, November 1. Very fine weather but frosty at night. George carting manure. Plasterers at Uncle George's. Our masons at James Woods. Library Reading Room open again in evening. We get the daily *[Leeds] Mercury.* All is very much in a muddle just now.

Monday, November 21. Forenoon at Fewston. Looked in at Inn and had two whiskys in company of Mr Wiseman, the Highways Surveyor. Talked with Vicar about proposed addition to churchyard. The present churchyard is full over and over again and the sights when digging graves are revolting.

Tuesday, November 22. Attended meeting of parishioners to consider adding ground to Fewston churchyard. Got put on committee to push the matter on.

Saturday, November 26. In the evening attended a concert at the Board School in Fewston which was got up by the Vicar's family in aid of church funds. A pretty good concert. Fanny sang a song but she was a poor singer as she lacks taste and time although she has not a bad voice, but she would try at this concert against my advice. But it got over and will soon be forgotten. Still, she did fairly well.

Saturday, December 3. A meeting of the committee in connection with the Reading Room at the Library. Resolved to vary the evening proceedings. Monday to be variety entertainment; Tuesday games; Wednesday reading exclusively; Thursday debate and discussion; Friday games and talk; Saturday reading. All full of hope that things will be more pleasant.

Tuesday, December 13. Found calf in mistal groop twelve weeks before time. A rather heavy loss as the cow will have to be kept over the time I purposed. I have been extremely unlucky in farming . . . the little land I have is worked at a loss and I should have been much better off if I had never known it.

Thursday, December 15. Evening discussion on the agricultural depression in the Reading Room. I stood up and made an address extempore. First I ever did and I think I did moderately well — at all events compared with the others.

Wednesday, December 21. Ceremony of planting memorial trees in the Library grounds. Mr Dearden, Robinson Gill's nephew over and planted a tree for Mr Gill and himself another. Several others planted memorial trees, including myself.

Sunday, December 25. Home most of Christmas Day. Chapel in the evening. Quiet for Christmas. Keen dry frost with clear starlit sky.

Sunday, January 1. The year 1892 is passed but by God's blessing I remain. We have had an exceptionally busy season with masons work and have worked it to a fair success, although we have suffered much through good masons being so hard to get . . . My expenses have been heavier this year. Of course our family has been more numerous and part extra outlay has been incurred so that in the gross I have expended about £2 10*s* a week on the average. So I will now leave the old year with its joys and sorrows and enter hopefully though soberly upon the work of another year. May He who watches over all things great and small be with me and those with whom I act and live.

1897

There is a second gap in the diaries, this time of five years, but since Dickinson gives no indication that he suspended his writing, it seems likely that the diaries for the intervening years have been lost. He is now 52 years of age, but in the past five years the pattern of his life has changed very little.

The year begins with a fine open day. I as usual have thoughts of trying to do more things . . . God spare me and help me to carry out any and all of my intentions for good. The world is far from perfect either in town or country and men and women need help to raise them from the degrading influences and habits to which they are so commonly subject.

As regards this immediate neighbourhood the state of the community is very dark and depressing. Farming is very unprofitable, the population is decreasing, the best families and the best men and women migrate to the towns. The consequence is that the hopeful zest and spirit which used to prevail 30 or 40 years ago is dead and life has become little more than a mere idle shuffle . . .

Friday, January 1. A little frost during the night and a nice bracing air and a pleasant drive to Otley. Called to register a birth at the workhouse and took the 11 train to Pool and registered a birth there. Back to Otley by 12.23 train. Paid James Whitaker my rent, registered two births at Pawsons and off home by 4.

Saturday, January 2. Had a walk with Dorothy round by Ridge Bottom and Ralph Wilsons. Dorothy enjoyed it very much.

Dorothy is now five years old.

Tuesday, January 7. Attended meeting of trustees of library at 2 o'clock. All the trustees and Uncle Dickinson sat down to a splendid dinner: roast turkey, sparerib of pork, rabbit pie, plum pudding, etc. Then had a few glasses of brandy and hot water after with social chat. We have taken to build a new house at Huby.

Saturday, January 9. Dressed and had good breakfast. Brother Charles went with me to the station. Snow falling fast. Called at Moons factory and spoke to Whitakers of Horsforth through a telephone.

Monday, January 18. Writing in parlour all day. Vicar of Burley-in-Wharfedale called in afternoon. Our men started for work at Weston. George took the horse and cart with tools. The gang consists of Cousin William Dickinson, nephews George and John Archer, Spence Ward and James Lister. It is a new departure and it may lead on to higher and broader success. As for me I don't look for much more mason work. I think I have had my day on the active list.

Tuesday, January 19. Nephew George went down to Huby and I am left to manage horse and cattle. I don't care for the work but I can do almost anything when I see it is required. Dorothy is not very well and we are a bit upset. Snow is hovering around.

Bleak and dreary are the days
Vain and foolish are our ways
Still we struggle with our fate
Hopes for better soon or late

Wednesday, January 20. Our little girl Dorothy does not recover as we should like. She is a very excitable child and how she will turn out we cannot divine. If she lives I think she will be a very lively sort of person.

Saturday, January 23. Dorothy broken out in measles, which makes us a little more settled as we now know what it is.

Wednesday, January 27. Up by 5.30. Dorothy very ill. Fanny had little sleep. I sleep in the other room now. We can only hope for the best and trust in God who is good . . . It is a right genuine old-fashioned winter. Mason and similar work at a standstill. I am somewhat upset in nerve and appetite all along. It is one of those dark periods which I suppose come to all lives at intervals.

Sunday, February 7. Not had a good night as the room I sleep in is cold. Must change back to wife as Dorothy is nearly well again . . .

Had roast pheasant to dinner, a present from Miss Snowden of Swinsty Hall. At no worship today. Must have given up that sort of thing, but it is so cold and dark.

Monday, February 8. Cousin William came up and we drove to Otley about 9. Saw Mr A. Marshall, the architect, and contracted for another new house to build at Weston. Attended at Dacres auction mart for an hour or two, also did various little jobs in the town . . . I am reading *Bleak House*. I think it is the best story I have read of Dickens.

Thursday, February 23. Reflecting a good deal on my present circumstances. We have a bit of dear land. The work occupies me a good deal, and I don't like the work. Besides there is no pay for it. I want to be out of it. Still, I don't like to part with the horse as it would be a step down to commence walking to Otley again. I would like to remove nearer Otley, but Fanny is opposed to it.

Thursday, February 25. At Moons at Fewston and at the Vicarage respecting little jobs we have there. Major Wilson is our mason up here just now. All the rest are down at Huby where we have two villas contracted for. George and John Archer, my nephews, are partners with us now.

Monday, March 1. Smoked two pipes of tobacco in the evening and was sick in consequence. I somehow cannot master smoking and I don't think I ever shall. I don't know whether to persevere or not as the habit at best is pernicious.

Generally the weather is most beastly
The wind is north or north-easterly
The birds, although it snows and blows,
Give voice, especially the crows
Which speaks that Spring will soon be here
And then our drooping hearts will cheer

Friday, March 5. We are planning to buy a little building ground at Huby with a view to building a few houses. It is a speculation . . . still, if nothing is done there is no success in anything.

Monday, March 8. Off to Huby by 7.30. Cousin William and George Archer rode along and we loosed out at Otley and took the 9.14 train to Weston. Met the Hutton brothers with a view to buying land to build houses upon. Did not agree as their price seems high for a country district.

Wednesday, March 17. Rumours of war about Crete. What will be the upshot of it no man can tell. The great Powers seem to be united but the sentiment of freedom is against them. There is no telling how far this may influence affairs. A good deal of despotism still exists in spite of the boasted liberties of the nations. Three pipes of tobacco today but not by any means master of it yet. Nature revolts against it I suppose. Perseverance may season me but it seems difficult.

> *The Cretan insurrection of 1896–97 led to war between Greece and Turkey which had held Crete since 1669. Greece was defeated, but the great Powers forced Turkey to evacuate Crete in 1898, and union with Greece was proclaimed in 1908.*

Thursday, April 1. Ice half an inch thick on our trough. I sent Bob Spence to Joe Holmes to ask for small end of North Pole. He ran off buoyantly and of course was rated an April Fool.

Wednesday, April 7. A fine morning. Frost abated. Attended to horse and bullock. Two lapwings eggs fried to breakfast. Very delicious. Jobbing about and reading daily *Mercury* up to noon. Afternoon digging the garden.

Sunday, April 11. Home all day until evening and then to church. Very cold inside and the sermon poor. No fire either in the stove or in the sermon. Mr Ashley the vicar is not a good man for the post and he gets worse.

> The April sun shines not
> Clouds gather all around
> Only in some favoured spot
> A flower may be found

Sunday, April 18. Fair all day for a wonder. Fanny reports that Joseph Holmes has got converted at the Wesleyan Chapel tonight. What that may be I cannot say.

Monday, April 19. Easter Monday. Sent bullock to auction. He was two years old on 25 March last and sold for £18 which is somewhat remarkable for a beast so young. A good many tourists through the village in wagonettes.

Wednesday, April 28. A pleasant Spring day, the cuckoo calling and all Nature budding forth into life. It is compensation for the gloom and darkness of the winter days.

Thursday, April 29. Busy gardening all day. Set potatoes and sowed onions radish lettuce and shallots as well as mowed lawn in front garden, so altogether very busy.

Thursday, May 6. Selected two hams and two flitches to exhibit at Otley Agricultural Show. They are not so nice as I would have liked and I am doubtful about getting a prize.

Friday, May 7. Otley Show. Large attendance. Got no prize.

Tuesday, June 22. Jubilee Day for Her Majesty Queen Victoria. Weather gloriously fine. Young folk mostly off to the towns . . . About 9.15 Fanny and I and Patty Holmes went up to Timble Ings to see the beacon fires. A good many others drew up on the same errand and we staied from 10 till 11. A fire of ling was kindled. We sang the National Anthem and had a fiddle and dancing. It was somewhat weird. Fireworks and beacon fires all around.

Tuesday, July 13. Everybody rushing into haytime like mad. Weather brisk with bright sunshine. Turned Field Syke and got Town End into large cock. Then put up Crooked Close into same and afterwards the whole of Field Syke. We used the hay sweep which helped a good deal.

Thursday, July 15. Carted remainder of hay in forenoon so we are the first to finish in Timble.

Monday, July 19. Jim Procter working for us today mowing thistles. Jim has had a wonderful career chiefly for drinking.

Monday, August 9. I am in the way of looking out for an investment in houses or land. I think I must try for something different from dreaming my time away in this sleepy village.

Tuesday, August 17. After tea I and my wife and Dorothy yoked up to drive to Bland Hill. In trotting along down North Lane the horse fell and my wife fell out on to the road and hurt herself, but not seriously, I think. But she and Dorothy turned back and I went on.

Wednesday, August 18. It is 22 years today since my dear father died. How swiftly time flies and how vain and fleeting are the things of life.

Thursday, August 19. Fanny stiff from her accident on Tuesday. About 4 o'clock a messenger arrived from Otley with a telegram as follows: 'Brooklyn, N.Y. to John Dickinson, Timble Great, near Otley, Yorkshire. Robinson Gill died sixteenth buried nineteenth, Frank Gill.' Fanny and I were deeply moved because we really loved the man. He was so simple and noble and good.

Monday, September 20. Off to Kettlesing by 8.30, cousin H. Procter with me. Got men fairly into work and hopes to push on successfully. Making up Parish Meeting accounts in evening for the audit.

> I drive in my trap over hill and through dale
> Through storm and in sunshine my movements don't fail
> To Saltergate Hill and to Kettlesing Head
> My journeys of late there have chiefly been sped
> In addition to Otley on Fridays I go
> And to Huby where business demands that I show

Sunday, September 26. Home all day until after tea. Then to Bill's at Gill Bottom. Back by Fewston. Called at Inn and had two whiskys. Wife grumbled when I got home at my drinking habits.

Monday, October 4. Very busy indeed here and there and am kept at a stretch. Still I find a little time to read Scott's *Heart of Midlothian.*

Friday, November 12. I am 53 years old today. Begins to feel old-manish but still I am flattered by constant remarks of how well and young-looking I am. Few I suppose would guess that I was over 50. When I look back what a host whom I knew who were to the front, full of hope and ambition, have now passed away. To me it seems a strange thing that man has much to learn before he can touch the fringe of the Great Mystery. All that has been said about a future life for man I believe to be merely the invention of man's mind, anxious for light on the mystery. Still I believe in the religion of doing right to my fellow men and trusting God for the rest.

Saturday, November 20. We are about finishing our main contracts off. I don't think the Weeton branch is likely to pay very well. Upon the whole we shall have a fair profit, but men are not as they used to be. They don't work so hard and the wages are very high.

Sunday, November 21. Through eating some pigs feet stew to supper and otherwise eating and drinking too much I was taken very ill through diarrhoea during the night and I did not go out all this day.

Monday, November 22. Much better in my health today. Towards evening got a good basin of oatmeal porridge and new milk.

Monday, December 13. Fanny went to Otley in afternoon. I was alone in the evening. Dorothy at her grandmothers. I should not like to fall back upon old bachelor days. Still there is a sort of freedom that one misses in this married life . . . Am reading *Our Mutual Friend* by Charles Dickens. Library is now well attended. Bagatelle playing every night which is very popular.

Thursday, December 21. Otley auction mart and prize day at Listers auctions. Harry Moss of Askwith had his purses stolen containing 30 sovereigns. Another man lost 17*s*6*d*, I feel tired of the long dreary journey over the moors betwixt here and Otley. I feel as if the time had come for me to remove my place of residence nearer to Otley. I have this on my mind, but then the Spring and summer come and the beauties of country life reconcile us to stay on at the old village home.

Thursday, December 23. Market day at Otley. I was there by 10.30. A glut of fat geese. Sparerib was very good to sell at eightpence a pound. Geese started at tenpence per pound but came down much lower. Everybody selling or buying for the coming festal season.

Saturday, Christmas Day. Very crisp dry frost. Dorothy up by daylight excited as to the work of Santa Claus. He had deposited several articles and she was highly delighted. Roast goose to dinner. Nephew George and niece Polly there.

Thursday, December 30. A public supper for residents in the Library district took place in the Library this evening. About 80 persons of all descriptions turned up. A 32-pound old ham and 20-pound of beef had been cooked, together with tarts, cheese, and spice cake, altogether making a capital feed. Dancing and singing was indulged in up to 2 a.m.

Friday, December 31. Another event at the Library. Seventy or 80 again sat down to supper. A sale of fragments fetched eight shillings.

So the year closes with its ups and downs, its joys and sorrows, and we are still among the living, fairly well and hopeful, but not carried away as formerly when the wild ambition of youth was full of dreams. My hopes are now tempered by knowledge gained from experience . . .

An event which deeply concerned me and which has affected the Timble people has been the death of that good man Robinson Gill. I had corresponded with Mr Gill for over 30 years and a bond of sympathy had grown up between us. I had been the medium through which he carried out his generous works both public and private in this district. He was looking forward to visiting the Old Country again next summer. Surely there must be some reward beyond this life for such a life's work as his. But there is no voice or sign to tell us for certain.

1898

The New Year opens finding me and mine in good health and hopeful for the future. I am not, it is true, feeling quite satisfied and content with things as they are. I have a strong impression that I don't get the good and pleasant things of life at Timble in the degree I might do if I lived, say nearer to Otley where the conveniences of modern civilisation are within easier reach. The journey to Otley is long and rough in the winter time and as the years pass I feel a desire to take things more comfortably. I feel the symptoms of the old man creeping upon me. I don't think I look so old as I am. Some men look quite in the sere and yellow leaf at 53, but I have only a little mixture of grey in my hair and whiskers. I wear my whiskers thus [*drawing of whiskered face in billycock hat*]; that is, I shave the chin and grow side whiskers and moustache which I clip rather short. I am still active and straight and when dressed up I look pretty smart. Still I have the premonition of old age coming on . . .

I look around at the hopeless struggle which the greater part of the people seem destined to wage barely to make a living. Then I look at those who are more successful and they too seem burdened and anxious lest their money should be lost or their trade fail. Then I look at the various religious sects and the strife and rivalry that prevails amongst them. The battle is going on in all classes of society. I am unable to satisfy my mind on what it all means. Ministers tell us of the consolation of religion. For my part I cannot get into the way of believing in the orthodox doctrines of Christianity. I think of the old dead religions of early civilisations. I read of the various religious faiths apart from Christianity and I am inclined to think that all religions have emanated from the heart and mind of man and that nobody in any age ever knew anything more than I do as to what follows after death.

Saturday, January 1. Festivities at the Library only broke up at three o'clock this morning so I have some excuse for lying late today. Attended meeting of Joint Burial Committee at Fewston Board School at 2 o'clock. I was appointed as one of a deputation to meet Leeds Waterworks Committee at Leeds to consult about a site for a burial ground. It is very shameful that the old churchyard should be closed and no steps yet taken to form a new ground.

Thursday, January 6. Cutting up a 37-stone pig in the forenoon. Meeting of the Library Committee at 3 p.m. and Trustees annual dinner at 4. The five Trustees and my Uncle George Dickinson and Mr Dearden over from Leeds to stay the night with us. At dinner roast turkey graced the table, plum pudding and roast beef. Spirits and cigars followed with social chat.

Sunday, January 9. Breakfast and then walk down into land. Mutton chops and plum pudding to dinner. Fanny at chapel afternoon and evening. She plays the harmonium.

Tuesday, January 11. Up by 8 and off to Harrogate to sign paper for contract for house at Huby for the Misses Lupton. Our contract is £505 for mason work, excavations and bricklayers work. The law now requires lamps on vehicles an hour after sunset, but I have not yet got any. Shall have to comply.

Saturday, January 15. Evening at Library. Appointed a lamplighter, Mrs Lister at one penny per night, commencing tomorrow evening.

Monday, January 17. Hung ten sides of bacon and ten hams. Evening at Library playing bagatelle. I am I think about as good at the game as anyone who attends.

Thursday, January 27. Cut up and salted two fat pigs. For the first time we left the spareribs in the flitch. We are trying it as an experiment. The old line of heavy fat pigs is going out of fashion and we must try for something to catch the market. Am reading Scott's *Bride of Lammermoor.*

Tuesday, February 1. Rough wild weather, but still no frost. Sent off rain guage returns.

Thursday, February 17. Planted rhubarb in mistal and put horse litter around it to force it. Expects it will come on early.

Sunday, February 20. Home all day. Reading a course of English history embracing the period of the rebellion in which the Charleses were so prominent.

Friday, February 25. Off to Otley by 8.30. Partly arranged for ground for a new house close to Weston Lane End, near Otley . . . Perhaps it is a bigger house or should be than we can aspire to reasonably, but we shall see. Now is the time or never . . . But when I come to face the matter I don't find it easy. Here I am fixed and possess some power and privilege that I would lose by removing. I cannot see my way clear.

Friday, March 11. Off to Otley by 9.30. Horse ran better than I ever knew it. A very fine day but one of those days when all looks against one: every hand, every face and every word feels to be against one.

Monday, March 21. George Archer drove me to Otley. I am turning over one bit of farming to him. I have made an offer for Sowerby Farm today: £1,000 practically allowing £200 for Maggie Tiplady's annuity of £8. I also made some arrangements respecting a proposed new house at Newall.

Thursday, March 24. A cold wild day and I am somewhat depressed. But sunshine and the song of birds and the bloom of flowers with all the bright things of Spring will renew my hopes in life. Annual Parish Meeting in the evening. I was reappointed chairman.

Monday, April 18. An improved postal service was started today. We now have letters delivered about 8.30 to 9 a.m. in place of 11 a.m.

Thursday, April 21. Setting a few early potatoes, and put in some shallots. Graving other parts of garden. A curious freak of Nature has occurred. A sow of Elijah Wards has had a litter of nine pigs and one of them had two heads, three eyes and six legs and two tails. It has only one trunk which divides into two hindparts with abdomen and all other hind parts entire.

Thursday, April 28. A contemporary of mine, Joseph Lister, about my age and a companion of my boyhood who used to be looked upon with envy as he had about £1,000 on attaining his majority and was a fine looking young man and a favourite of the females, is now over at Timble penniless and a wreck physically.

Monday, May 2. Wife and I at Otley in afternoon. Fanny went about a costume but I am sure I don't know what the word means. I had business respecting our proposed new house at Newall. I think it is a step in the right way but can't be sure.

Tuesday, May 3. Much talk and newspaper reports of war betwixt the United States and Spain. Hostilities have already commenced.

> *Partly brought about by the repressive Spanish administration in Cuba. When the U.S. battleship Maine was destroyed in Havana with the loss of 260 of her crew, outraged American opinion assumed the Spaniards had blown it up. The U.S. declared war and when peace was signed in Paris in December 1898 the Americans gained control of the Philippines, Guam island and Puerto Rico. Spain also ceded Cuba pending a declaration of an independent republic.*

Wednesday, May 11. A wild windy wet day. Not at all cuckoo weather but he sings cheerfully for all that. Preparing Poor Rate most of the day.

Saturday, June 11. Funeral of Rhodes Renton, or Newsom. Took trap to Weston. Jos. Holmes and my sister Mary Ann Archer rode with me. A cold north wind but very hot in the sun down Askwith way. Two cabs and the hearse and about seven traps. Most of the people rode. Ham and beef tea at the Black Horse at Askwith.

Tuesday, June 21. Off to Huby by 7 then to Otley and met Mr Palliser and Mr Fawkes at Pool Old Mills to look at the old mill wall stones with a view to pulling down. Tea at cousin Harry Procters then off home. A miserable wet journey though I was jolly enough reciting Tennyson's *Charge of the Light Brigade*, etc. I sometimes amuse myself whilst driving across the moors reciting pieces.

Thursday, June 23. Wife and I drove to Otley. Jos. Holmes drove trap back to Timble and we took 10.59 train to Leeds, Harry Procter and his wife with us. After dinner at the Turks Head Hotel we took train for Cardigan Field where Barnum and Baileys *Greatest Show on Earth* was performing. The attendance was a record over 14,000 and the performance was marvellous in its magnitude variety and perfection.

Tuesday, July 19. We have finished leading hay and I am very glad as it is very hard work. Yoked up horse and trap about 11 and drove to Harrogate to see about material for a job of mason work we have in hand at Killinghall Lane End. Fell in with very jolly company. Heard a graphophone I think it is called that reproduced songs.

Friday, July 22. At Otley. Took copies to the superintendent registrar. Met Dr Collyer and walked round town with him. He called to see his old shop mate Joe Mason who worked with him 60 years ago in the blacksmiths shop at Ilkley. It was very pleasant to hear them talk in the old broad dialect, and Collyer so tender and sympathetic. At parting he said, 'Thoul want a bit o' beef Joe this Feeast', and gave him a sovereign.

Thursday, July 28. About 11 o'clock Fanny fell ill and after calling in her mother and Mrs Lister she had a miscarriage she being about two months gone with child. I have mixed feeling at this event. One would like Nature to have its course and if it had been a boy it might have kept up the name.

Monday, August 1. Very quiet Feast at Timble. Many villagers off to Otley. Mr Gill's donation missed this year.

Tuesday, August 16. Up by 6.30. Forenoon fitting up Library for the Robinson Gill Memorial service. A fine warm day. There was a large attendance, many from a distance. Dr Collyer said just what ought to be said about the life and character of Mr Gill, and he said it so feelingly and eloquently.

Tuesday, August 23. To Farnley and Otley. I am almost tired of driving about constantly, but the air is sweet and pure and the prospect is charming crossing the moors and the meadows are a rich deep green and the woods and fields present a pleasing variety of colour that cannot be equalled at any other season of the year.

Wednesday, August 24. Home in forenoon writing. Dinner with green peas, own growing. Delicious. Bacon and apple pudding. After dinner yoked trap and drove to Killinghall Lane. George working there. All going on well. Had tea at the Travellers Inn.

Wednesday, August 31. We are building the new school at Farnley. My nephews John and George Archer are in charge of the masons work. If they get through with it I shall be very glad as I feel I want to leave off the leading responsibility. Back to Otley and staied a while at Weston Lane End where masons are engaged building a house for me. Changes seem to be coming round which I trust will develop to meet my aspirations to a higher life than this present circle affords.

Tuesday, September 6. George Dickinson and Polly Archer got married today. Quite a stir in the village. Bride and bridegroom and party drove to Ilkley. Evening dancing in the Library. George is my cousin and Polly is my niece. I don't care for this marrying relations but it seems to be inevitable sometimes.

Thursday, September 8. Met the revising barrister at the Court House in Otley with lists of voters. All passed off very well and I got about £2 out of the job.

Thursday, September 15. Weighed seven hams and took them in trap for the landlord of the White Hart at Pool, price 9½*d* per lb. Went by our new house in course of erection at Weston Lane End, then drove up to Farnley and looked over work we have in hand building a new school. Drove on to Pool and had dinner there and a glass of beer, then drove to Otley and baited.

Friday, September 23. Took deeds of my house in Station Road, Otley, to manager of Yorkshire Bank as security in case I overdraw at the Bank during the next few months.

Monday, September 26. Nutting with wife. Very fine dry weather.

Tuesday, September 27. Drove to Otley and went to Mr Cowling in Gay Lane. Agreed with Mrs Cowling for Sowerby Farm to buy it, giving her £200 and taking over £700 mortgage and paying £8 annuity to Maggie Tiplady during her life. It is the most important transaction that I ever entered upon.

Monday, October 3. Went to J.W. Yeadons at Fewston first thing. George drove and the horse stumbled and fell and knocked skin off its knees. Drove on to Fewston and bathed and washed them and put on gunpowder and lard . . . Am reading life of the poet Pope.

Friday, October 14. I am immersed in a good deal of transactions just now. First, I am building a new house at Weston Lane End which may cost about £700. Second I have bought Sowerby Farm at Four Lane Ends, Timble and the deeds are now being prepared. I give £900 and pays Margaret Tiplady, a woman of about 20, an annuity for her life of £8 per annum. £700 is on mortgage at 3 per cent so that I am only £200 out at present. Mason work and bacon curing fill up my time, so that I am a rather busy man.

Wednesday, November 2. The dull days are upon us. Bother about Library Endowment Fund. The Denver Paper Mill Company in which Mr Gill invested it has defaulted and we are likely to have a good deal of trouble if not loss.

Tuesday, November 8. Drove to Otley. My business was to complete the purchase of Sowerby Farm which was completed at Mr Barrett's office. I am now become a landed proprietor and consequently must stand somewhat higher in the social scale.

Monday, November 14. In the evening a sort of social concert at the Library. Songs and recitations. I sang The Farmer's Boy and it was well received. I think I did it very well to say that I don't profess to be much of a singer. I think I am very tuneable and can sing with some taste. I have a bass voice, fairly sweet but not powerful.

Friday, November 18. The Statutes at Otley. Much drinking and foolishness among the young folk. I left soon after 4. I have no pleasure in the low public house company. I agree with Carlyle that most folk are fools amongst which I include myself although age and experience have somewhat sharpened my wits or else dulled my passions so that I am now a more sober and sensible man than I used to be at the Statutes long since gone by.

Wednesday, December 14. George started for Otley about 2 o'clock to meet Fanny who has been to Leeds today to attend a sort of musical examination. Fanny perseveres very hard in music but I fear she lacks the natural gift and I don't think she will ever excel.

Sunday, Christmas Day. Only a few boys round with the usual Christmas greetings. And not so early as usual. We used to be out two hours before daylight and great was the racket and excitement. What changes since then. Roast goose to dinner. Harry Procter and George Archer here to dine. Tea at Aunt Mary's.

Tuesday, December 27. Terribly wet windy morning. A regular hurricane and flood. Cleared up towards evening. The chapel folks held a public tea party in the Library and a magic lantern performance followed, entitled Religious Progress.

Wednesday, December 28. Unsettled about various matters, but the one main question is whether to go to live at the new house I am building at Newall. I really think it would be the best thing to do, but one is rooted in various ways to the old home and how the cat will jump I am unable to say. I trust to that Providence which has generally guided me to a fair degree of success so far. May he whose all seeing eye sweeps the universe watch and guide me . . .

1899

The year opens with plenty of work waiting for me . . . I am not so energetic as I used to be, but still I can do a good deal of useful work if I am spared in health and lays aside a tendency to indolence . . . We talk of removing Otley way. If we do that new influences and new associations will surround us . . . but a residence of over 54 years cannot be changed without serious thought and some misgivings. But then we should hardly be amongst strangers. We know and are known to almost everybody in Otley and district and on market day old familiar faces will turn up as sure as the sun.

Sunday, January 1. Preacher to tea. In house all day. Cooked dinner. Wife teaching at Sunday School. Came on snow and very rough night.

Monday, January 16. Weather wild and dirty. Over at Major Wilsons in the evening. Major is a very careful man and they sit without light and very little fire in the evening. It is one way of saving money. I don't care for that way so we keep up good fires and plenty of light and our house looks cosy and comfortable.

Sunday, January 22. Wet and wild again. Am reading Bret Harte's *Gabriel Conroy*. Good warm potato pie to dinner. Preacher to tea, a Mr Ritchie of Otley. Attended evening service at chapel. Horse still out of sorts but mending.

Saturday, January 28. I am almost fully employed writing every day now. The book-keeping becomes more and more particular. The outlook for work is very good. Building seems to be developing on every hand. All the towns seem to be spreading. When it will stop no one knows, but no doubt a slump will follow. I am somewhat drawn into the vortex of this speculative mania. House at Otley cost £600. Building house at Newall cost nearly £700. Farm at Sowerby cost £1,100 so I am getting well into the lists. I trust it will all turn out well . . . Reading Abraham Lincoln's Life. A very wonderful man, sent by God for a purpose.

Tuesday, February 7. The ground covered with snow. Indoors I have been very comfortable, a good fire and writing vaccination business. My good wife has cooked meals of inviting and nutritious quality. Our little girl Dorothy is all about commanding our attention . . .

Thursday, February 16. Weather better and the country places begin to look brighter. Birds sing in the woods and fields. The first little sights and sounds of Spring begin. It is a bright and hopeful old world after all its gloom and cares. The song of a bird, the peep of a flower, and above all the heavenly look of a pretty sweet-faced girl makes us forget sorrows.

Tuesday, February 21. Much talk about a shooting match for £10 betwixt John Taylor of Scow Hall, Norwood, and one Benson of Addingham. Benson won. There is a mania just now for pigeon shooting and many are following it that might very well find more profitable employment. It is nothing but an excuse for idleness.

Saturday, March 6. My daily business is very mixed. First there is the mason business as a partner with cousin William Dickinson, now of Huby, and my two nephews John and George Archer. I find the money but does not do actual labour. I get one-third of the profits. The business is mostly at Huby and some in this district. Secondly, I am registrar and vaccination officer for the Fewston district. Three, I am a farmer of seven acres. Four, I am a partner with cousin Andrew Dickinson in salting 20 to 30 fat pigs. I find the money. Five, I am an acting overseer this year. Six, I am the attendant on the rain guage for Leeds Corporation. Seven, I am the waterworks superintendent for Timble supply. Eight, Secretary of the village club. Nine, Chairman and clerk of the Parish Meeting. Ten, I am trustee and clerk of the Robinson Library and Free School. Eleven, I am a reporter for the *Otley Observer.* Twelve, Agent for fire insurance. Thirteen, Agent for a manure company.

Thursday, March 23. Scarce possible to remain out of doors, so very keen and cold it is. Attended annual Parish Meeting, and was appointed assistant overseer at a salary of £6 per year.

Wednesday, April 19. Wife assisted by Emma Wilson, daughter of Major Wilson, cleaning down. Spring cleaning. It is a bother. Went down to Mr Bramleys at Swinsty Hall and sat for an hour or two. Mr Bramley is a bachelor of some 54 years. He has a housekeeper, Miss Snowden, some 30 years old who rules a good deal but she acts very well for him and makes him comfortable. Whether the relationship is simply that of master and servant I don't know, but one might think that a man and maid alone together are a mixy quantity.

Thursday, April 27. At Sowerby Farm all day. G. Archer, Alf Dickinson and Willy Margerisson working there. Pulled the front down. It is a very wide old wall, built 226 years ago when Charles the Second was holding his merry court. About this period many good houses were built in this district and it must have been a time of great prosperity.

Sunday, April 30. Church in evening. Several months since I was at church. Cannot stand the cold damp seats.

Tuesday, May 9. Am exceedingly hard run now with various business and things are not at all pleasant. To add to other griefs Fanny is busy cleaning down.

Wednesday, May 24. Queen Victoria 80. Good old Queen. Her public and private virtues shine forth strongly in contrast to past monarchs. Public tea at the chapel.

Friday, July 28. Off to Otley by 9, sister Mary Ann and Aunt Mary with me. I had applied for the office of Plans Surveyor to the Wharfedale Rural District Council, but feeling somehow down and doleful I wrote a letter withdrawing my application and I delivered it at the Union offices. Afterwards I saw Mr Hornsby Jackson the chairman of the Council, and Mr Exley of Menston and they both pressed me to come forward for the post and I did so and got the appointment.

Wednesday, August 2. Haymaking in full swing. Everybody overdone. The heat is really something awful. I have kept loitering about with no heart for anything. The sultry air is like an oven, and all Nature seems oppressed. Strong men swelter under the sun's hot rays and weaker folk sink over-powered. O, for a drenching rain to cool the parched earth and give life to weary Nature.

Thus we toil on the seasons round
The question rises Whither bound?
Toil and trouble is our lot
And soon we leave all we have got
The fleshly man seeks pleasures gay
Whilst wiser folk do watch and pray
Which way is right I want to know
That I may tell what seeds to sow

Sunday, August 20. Church in evening. I think our Vicar, Mr Ashley, does not give the consideration to his sermons that he did formerly. He seems to think any unconsidered remarks good enough for the people of this isolated parish, but dull as we are we can see through our wily parson and rate him at his true worth.

Wednesday, September 13. The slaters are at work covering the barn at Sowerby Farm and I am kept on the look-out seeing that the work is well done. Workmen are very careless now and they will not take pains as they used to do. The world has quite changed since my early days. Wages have increased and the working man is very much better off than formerly. Whether this will continue is another question. Maybe decline will set in in course of time and England, like the ancient empires of the past will decline and fall and new empires arise.

Saturday, September 16. At Sowerby in forenoon. Weather very dry. Rain much wanted. The world wags its way. The Dreyfus case in France and the Transvaal question are to the front as public matters. For myself the question as to whether I should leave Timble is foremost.

> *Alsatian Jewish Captain Alfred Dreyfus, court-martialled in 1894 for treason by giving military information to the Germans was sentenced to imprisonment on Devil's Island, but three years later a Major Esterhazy was named as the traitor. Dreyfus's cause was taken up by the novelist Emile Zola with a famous challenge to the authorities, J'Accuse, and Dreyfus was retried in 1899. He was found guilty with extenuating circumstances, but the public outcry continued, and in 1906 the verdict was quashed. Dreyfus was re-admitted to the army, promoted, served with distinction in World War I and lived until 1935.*

Saturday, September 23. The gales are upon us. Not so buoyant in spirits. Wet day.

> Toil and worry year in year out
> I wonder what it's all about
> The birth, the prime and then the grave
> There's nothing more for prince or knave

Saturday, September 30. John Archer my nephew and Lena Dale got married at Fewston Church today. Fanny somewhat offended at the manner of our invitation and we did not go. These matters are only trivial and will look very poor as the years go by.

Monday, October 2. I don't shoot pheasants or in fact anything. My father was a keen shooter and never tired of ranging the woods and fields for game. But I soon found out it was not a paying thing so I did not take it up. But as I advance in years I see that there are other things worth doing besides making money and I often envy the happy, light-hearted times my father must have had with his dog and gun.

Tuesday, October 3. Off to Middleton near Ilkley by 7.30. Inspected three new villas there for Messrs Dean Brothers, then drove to Ilkley and Burley and Menston to inspect other buildings. Drove home in a rough blast of wind. Evening a social gathering at the Library. I sang 'The Good Rhein Wine' with fair effect, but not to my mind as I was nervous. Later I recited 'The Charge of the Light Brigade' by Tennyson. This also with fair effect but both much short of what I should wish and feels competent for with good training.

Wednesday, October 18. Up by 7.30. We indulge more than we ought in lying in bed. Washed and had oatmeal porridge to breakfast. Then the *Yorkshire Post* newspaper came with news of the Transvaal War and the defeat of Sir Thomas Lipton's yacht in one of the races for the Americas Cup.

> *The Transvaal War was really the second Boer War in which Britain annexed the Transvaal for the second time. But between 1899 and January 1900 there were a series of Boer successes in which British garrisons were besieged in Ladysmith, Mafeking and Kimberley.*
> *America's Cup, named for the America, the yacht which defeated British craft in 1851. Yachting enthusiast Sir Thomas Lipton (1850–1931) made five unsuccessful attempts to win the Cup.*

Wednesday, November 1. Much excitement and chagrin is felt just now at the humiliating news from the seat of war in South Africa where our soldiers have suffered a very humiliating reverse. It seems to have been a blundery affair. This war is assuming gigantic proportions and we are not finding it so easy to carry our point. Eventually we must win if none of the great Powers intervene but it is likely to be a terrible sacrifice in blood and treasure.

> *Some compensation began in February 1900. In the period up to August British counter-offensive under Lord Roberts led to the relief of the garrisons and the occupation of the Boer capital, Pretoria in June. The war ended in May 1902.*

Wednesday, November 15. Wife and Lotty Holmes cleaning down. Dorothy at school under Miss Stevens. The Library Endowment Fund is likely to fail and the outlook is rather serious as the school will have to be closed unless the full value of the bonds we hold is realised, which now seems to be very doubtful . . . Salted fat pig that I bought of George Dickinson of Sowerby Farm. It is for our own use. I am going out of the bacon salting business. I have been in it for close on 40 years. It has brought in a profit every year, sometimes over £20 but mostly an average of say £12 . . . It is not a very certain business and is a declining trade.

Saturday, November 18. Up by 7 and off to Newall. A weasel had just killed a rabbit in Snowden Bank and I got the rabbit. This is the second rabbit at the same place in the past two weeks. Loosed out at Roebuck Inn and walked to Farnley and paid men there. Nine are at work. Back to dinner at the Roebuck. Said rabbit stewed and very nice.

Saturday, December 2. Paid men at Mount Pleasant and Herrickstones Farm on Farnley estate. Loosed out at Richard Holmes and had dinner there. Dick drunk.

Saturday, December 16. The nation is staggered by news of further reverses in the Transvaal. We feel humiliated as a nation and perhaps we deserve it. We have been too haughty and boastful. General Buller on whom the hopes of the campaign rested has tried his hand and failed. There is surely something queer about it and the fate of the Empire seems to hang in the balance.

Friday, December 22. Began snowing about 9 o'clock. Fanny had intended going to Otley but gave it up. Sister with me there. Bought fat goose on the Cross of William Mudd of Slade House, Thornthwaite. Weighed 12 pounds and paid 10½*d* a pound for it. It looks a lot of money but Christmas only comes once a year and we might as well try to enjoy ourselves.

Saturday, December 23. Busy sweeping snow off walks for an hour or two. The days are short now and we light our 50-candlepower lamp about 3 o'clock so that our main recreation consists in the evening variety such as reading and writing.

Monday, Christmas Day. A very cold morning. A good many boys round with their greetings, one or two before daylight. We gave several threepence each, some twopence and the rest a penny. We had roast goose to dinner.

Sunday, December 31. The year and the century have come to a close. The century is too big a matter for me to dwell on, the year I can in some measure grasp . . . The closing months found old England in face of a very grave crisis. The Transvaal War is taxing the resources of the country. There has never been such a call upon the nation in my time.

Personally the past year has favoured me with fairly good health and apparent prosperity. I have built a new house at Weston Lane End, Newall, which is let at £30 a year. I have spent a great amount of time at Sowerby Farm superintending alterations to the house and buildings. I have got another appointment under the Wharfedale District Council as Inspector of Plans and Buildings. The job suits me very well so far.

May God grant his help and support in any work I may undertake in the coming year.

1900

The year opens overshadowed by dark clouds for England, but the watchword is Onward to Conquer. So it is with me. I feel hemmed in with clouds, real or imaginary . . . But the steady sun of hope shines behind the clouds and I trust that these dark days will pass over . . . I am getting too old to make much headway in the face of sharp competition, but I feel disposed to keep pegging at it as long as I comfortably can.

Monday, January 1. Public supper at the Library. About 100 sat down to 46lbs of old ham boiled, which was very good, beef and other good things. A dance followed. The young folk enjoyed themselves, the usual love-making and flirtations going on. It was ever so. I still figure in these events with a sort of distinction. I play the violin some whilst my wife presides at the piano. Held out until 2 in the morning.

Tuesday, January 9. Better news from the seat of war. Ladysmith still stands. The days are getting a little longer and hope brightens as they do so. My new Mackintosh is a most capital thing for a wet drive, keeps one warm and dry.

Tuesday, January 16. Fanny and I went down to Fewston. I called on William Beecroft to pay him School Board call and collect rate. Fanny went on to the Vicarage for certificates of marriages. We both had supper at Joseph Moons. Fewston is becoming a dilapidated place. Once it was a busy prosperous village. Now there are only a few old folk and no laughter of children is to be heard.

In the rest of January and most of February Dickinson goes about his newly-added task of planning and buildings inspector, selling his horse for £24 and buying a pony and lighter trap for his travelling. He moans about his health, his business worries, the Boer War, the gloomy prospect for

Library funds, and a spell of wild winter weather that cuts off the villages with deep snow. But he is cheered by news of the relief of Kimberley and in March by the relief of Ladysmith, most of all by the first signs of Spring in the Washburn valley.

Tuesday, March 6. Walked to Otley and met George Carver. Took a house in terrace near Otley Bridge. It seems a great wrench for us to leave Timble, but the drive to Otley from Timble is now too much for me in rough weather and I cannot stand it.

> The days are getting longer but the cold is still severe
> The birds are a-singing on every bough which is good cheer
> The farmers men are busy leading out manure
> And the summer is a-coming with balmy breezes pure
> Rejoice O man with birds and beasts at the voice of Spring
> Give praise to God above and hallelujahs sing
> Surely the voice of Spring bespeaks a power divine
> That leads to goals of goodness, so why should we repine?

Tuesday, March 27. Drove to Otley and took 10.59 train to Leeds and went to Mr Beevers office to sign contract for farm buildings at Pool Hall. Contract £760 . . . nearly £100 higher than the next highest tender. No doubt we stand well in reputation for making good work, otherwise we should not have got the job . . .

Sunday, April 1. At no place of worship, but in house reading and then a walk out enjoying the beauty of Creation. In what better way can we worship God?

Tuesday, April 3. Up by 6.30. Broiled a good mutton chop cut through the leg and with coffee made a capital breakfast.

Thursday, April 5. George Archer walling garden wall in front of Mr Gowlands house, the topmost house going out of high end of the village. Meeting of Library trustees at 3 o'clock. The endowment fund is a failure.

Saturday, April 7. Wrote to the Rev. Robert Collyer about our Library. We are having scarcely any income now and we are anxious to know what is to be done about the Denver Paper Mill in which the money is invested. I fear most of it will be lost.

Sunday, April 8. Fanny and I at church. Had talk with the Vicar.

Church affairs are very cold. The family is at Harrogate all along and the Vicarage is shut up. Mr Ashley is a very poor man for a rural parish, and his wife is also unsuitable being rather flighty in her mind. Mr Ashley is a fine classical scholar and can talk well but that is not what is wanted here.

Saturday, April 14. Evening meeting to raise funds for carrying on the Library school. About £15 promised to keep the school going.

Wednesday, April 25. Off to Harrogate by 9.30. Drove by way of Kettlesing Head. Met cousin William and discussed business matters. The Hotel Majestic is building and it is to be opened on June 1. It is the largest and noblest hotel in the town. Truly Harrogate has developed wonderfully this last decade. Trade is a wonderful thing for making money and the smoky towns of the West Riding make wealthy men come and build fine houses at such places as Harrogate.

Wednesday, May 2. Afternoon up at Sowerby Farm and drew £21 of George Dickinson, my tenant, for the last Martinmas rent. Home in evening. Boiled onions to supper.

Sunday, May 6. A wet wild day. At no worship again. I must mend my ways.

> An active life, so thinks my wife
> She tells me I've too much in hand
> And maybe lose both house and land
> But I think that by persevering
> I will keep the vessel steering
> And everything will come out right
> If I make a gallant fight

Monday, May 7. Yoked about 3.30 and drove to Otley. Called on H. Procter and had tea and brought over 30 newly-hatched chickens to Aunt Mary's. A most beautiful day.

Sunday, May 20. Pleasant walk out in the Spring sunshine amongst the flowers and birds. This I must set up as my form of worship. I love the quiet lanes and solitary woods. What I shall do when I get close to Otley I cannot say.

Thursday, May 31. Very cold and growth slow. Sold trap to Fred Lister for £13. Fred is coming to reside at Timble. Joe Holmes is again wrong in his mind, a very queer case.

Tuesday, June 5. A good muster of Club members. The Rawdon Band of Music arrived about 10.30 and the procession started to Fewston. Mr Storey of the Waterhouse came out and announced that he had just received a telephone message from Otley that Lord Roberts had entered Pretoria. The procession pulled up and the band played God Save the Queen.

Monday, July 2. At home packing things for our intended removal to Newall. It is a very upsetting business and I shall be glad when it is over. One wants to be young to brave this kind of work, but it is now or never and I really think it is the proper thing to do. Nephew George will take up our home in Timble and I suppose will carry on much as we have done.

Wednesday, July 4. Walter Roundell came with three wagons and the loading was tackled about 9 o'clock. All was loaded by 3 and the wagons started off. G. Archer, myself wife and Lotty Holmes followed in the trap. The unloading was very heavy work and we were all thoroughly tired. We improvised beds on the spring mattresses and so slept very comfortably in our new home. This is an important change. The main object is to cut the journeys from Timble to Otley which have got to outface me of recent years. Almost all my business lies in the Otley centre and I felt out of the run of things whilst I remained in Timble. Still Timble has its advantages. There is the beautiful scenery and the pure air.

Thursday, July 5. First night in our new home with all things fresh and the upset complete. When we shall get to feel settled and comfortable is a problem for the seers and prophets.

Friday, July 6. Popped over into town and got shaved. Felt rather lost in the new order of things.

Friday, July 13. Crossed over to Otley in good time — very different from having to journey all the way from Timble, but this fine weather makes one feel to want the drive over the moor to breathe the pure fresh air, but here we are now and must take the better with the worse and hope it will be mostly better . . . One almost doubts whether we have done the right thing. Our way lies through clouds of doubt and fear, but all my little successes in life have been carried out with fear and trembling as it were. But I always suffer more or less in hot weather.

Wednesday, July 25. Took 11 train to Leeds to sign contract at

Weeton House. Had dinner at Brayshaw's — salmon, for the first time in my life. At Pool the other day. We have about 15 men at work there paying them about £20 a week.

Sunday, August 19. Church in evening. Mr Ashley's farewell sermon. Very affecting. The Vicar wept and so did we. Twenty-seven years is a long time and we had known him closely.

Saturday, August 25. Washed and dressed and attended the Friendly Societies' fête. Grand procession through Otley. Band contest in cricket field and other attractions. Went to theatre in evening.

Wednesday, August 29. At workhouse registering two deaths. One was that of King Grange, late of Timble. Poor King, a man of very robust constitution fallen through drink and women . . . Fanny seems unhappy. Fact is she is not really well and her temper is ruffled in consequence.

Tuesday, September 11. Up early. Fanny and I and brother Charles and his wife all got ready. I met Jesse Crabtree at Menston who had a smart horse and trap and we drove direct to Kilnsa. The weather was glorious, the scenery the same, and I never enjoyed a journey so much. Bro. Charles and Fanny went by train to Skipton and took bus forward. Rest of the day at Kilnsa where the show was in progress, with the grand old Crag looming over the scene and the surrounding beautiful scenery. Everybody from miles around seemed to be there. Sports followed the show. A race was run up to the top of the Crag and back. It was a fearful job getting up and still more the breakneck coming down but no accident happened. At about 8 took the bus up to Kettlewell with Mr Ottiwell Robinson whose guests we were during our stay. A most hospitable gentleman and a fine man in every sense.

Wednesday, September 12. Up by 7. A glorious morning. Good breakfast and then a walk up the foot of Whernside. Then by trap to Hubberholme Church, a venerable shrine which speaks of a life we cannot now quite realise with our new developments. Buckden was preparing for its annual sheep fair. The scenery is weird and romantic. Back to Kettlewell to dinner and a look round the church and village. Had walk up road towards Moor End Farm. About 43 years ago I walked up the same road to this farm and staied all night there. What changes since then. A cup of tea with Mr Robinson's housekeeper and we took the mail bus at 4.20 p.m. for Skipton. It was crowded to capacity. With many varying incidents and good company we arrived at Skipton about 7 o'clock, then train to Shipley and forward to Otley by the 8.55 train. And so home, pleased with the outing.

Sunday, September 16. Evening at chapel. I don't care for the Wesleyan service. Somehow there seems a lot of starch and buckram all round.

Saturday, September 22. Train to Harrogate and on to Oatlands where we have two villas building. We have too much on hand. Home by noon. George Archer met us with trap and and we all went to Timble. The drive was refreshing, the air is more bracing on the hills. The old village very quiet. Not sure I have done wisely to leave . . . My wife complains of being lonely. We have not formed any social connections yet in the town.

Tuesday, October 9. After tea my wife and I walked over to Farnley, visiting the church. A very fine evening. We enjoyed the walk as it seemed to bring back old associations of country life. We are children of the open fields and woods and love the song of birds and the scent of wild flowers, with nuts and blackberries as they come in season.

Wednesday, October 10. All excitement about the election. Mr Wyvill the Conservative candidate, Mr Duncan the Liberal. The crowds were dense in the evening when the ballot boxes came in. Around the maypole an immense throng assembled in which I and my wife occupied a place close to the maypole railings. For three mortal hours we waited for the declaration. This came about 1 o'clock, Duncan being declared elected by a large majority. Then much noise at the clubs.

The General Election confirmed the Unionists (Conservatives) in office with a majority of 134, the Marquess of Salisbury remaining Prime Minister.

Monday, November 5. Evening at the workhouse, Fanny, Dorothy and I. A big bonfire was lit and an effigy of Kruger was burned and a large quantity of fireworks were let off. We were invited inside and partook of the hospitality of the Master and Mistress.

Thus our days pass at the house near the town
Sometimes fortune smiles and sometimes it will frown
The dirt has been fearful but now it is better
But for all that I'm thinking of writing a letter
To the paper to tell of the region we live
And to ask if the Council can't improvements give

Thursday, November 22. Breakfast and then read paper. Took train to Ilkley and visited houses at Middleton, then home to tea.

Weather dull and dirty, spirits rather down
Noise of life and merriment over in the town
Couples bent on courting stroll on Farnley Lane
And tell the old old story which is fresh though told again
Thus ever round and round the circling years speed by
And Time its impress makes although to check it we may try

Saturday, November 24. Up to Farnley where we have men at work. All going on seemingly well.

Cold and frost will soon be here
And Christmas time with lots of cheer
Roaring fire and warmth within
Pleasures plenty if you've the tin
But woe betide the poor and needy
The cold will make them feel more seedy

Monday, December 3. We feel somewhat dull as yet having made few friends here. Still I think we should not like to go back to Timble although the memory of happy times there will ever be dear to us. But we were younger then and what memories are like those of youth? Planted rose tree in front garden. Wet again in evening. Wharfe very full.

As I went over Otley brig
A man dashed past me in a gig
He whipped his horse with might and main
He wanted to get through the rain
And so he made the poor horse suffer
For fear the weather would get rougher

Friday, December 21. Preparations for Christmas are active.

Shopkeepers striving to catch the public eye. As yet this activity is new to us. The old quiet village life is still in our hearts and the noise and bustle and apparent heartlessness of town life jars on our nerves, used as they have been to the quiet ways of Timble. Over in town I bought a fat goose, 9½lbs at 10½*d* per lb. Also bought one at 10*d* per lb weighing 11lbs to send over to Timble.

Tuesday, Christmas Day. We missed the usual early morning salute. Boys came but in another manner, knocked at the door first and then told their tale. We had roast goose to dinner but only ourselves to eat it.

The early months of the past year brought some very rough wintery weather and crossing the moors Otley way and back mostly twice a week caused me to consider whether it was best to continue to brave the moors or to move near to Otley. I decided in favour of removing and on 4 July we moved to Newall Mount Terrace. The weather was very hot for the first month or so. We did not like it at all and longed for the bracing fresh breezes of Timble. But as colder weather came we settled down more comfortably. But I don't think we have yet fairly settled to the new conditions. We have been used to village life throughout our lives and coming here seemed to cut us off from home intercourse and the old familiar ways and folk. This is what we miss. But in all other ways we are much better living here. As regards my registration business it is much more convenient. My duties as building inspector I could hardly have carried on without coming nearer to Otley. Another thing is the education of our little girl Dorothy. We think there is a better chance of her getting some refinement of manners which was not to be looked for at Timble. And lastly I was getting to the verge of oldmanhood and did not feel able to face the blasts and the long journeys driving on cold wet days.

1901

Looking forward to the New Year and the new century influenced by subdued and humble aspirations. The weight of 56 years tell me I am no longer young . . . I feel the creep of age . . . and yet I am not quite cast down. I have a calm resolve to do some good things if I am spared . . . The conditions of my life and business must undergo changes during the coming year . . .

I am purposing practising more economy. The past year has been very expensive. In the meantime I trust that God in his providence will watch over us and give us peace of mind and business prosperity.

Tuesday, January 1. This first day of the year finds me very lonely having nobody but myself in the house. Fanny and Dorothy are over at Timble. It was well on in the forenoon before I got breakfast, then I had to cook dinner — roast sparerib and potatoes.

Wednesday, January 2. Still alone up to 7.30. Writing most of the day.

The war still keeps our minds disturbed
John Bull's abused with spite uncurbed
And England seems to stand alone
Whilst other nations hoot and groan
Because we colonise so much
And take the power from the Dutch

Friday, January 11. Am very comfortable but not yet broken off the old country ways with the wild freedom of the ghylls and lanes and fields. Received by this mornings post a draft for £410 from the Rev. Robert Collyer of New York for the Library and school at Timble. It is the gift of a rich and generous friend of Mr Collyer and a right royal gift too. We are in luck. I was down and now am raised.

Monday, January 21. Queen's illness is the chief topic of conversation today.

Tuesday, January 22. Death of the Queen. The news arrived in Otley about 8. Much sympathy. People really sorry. My wife shed tears moved by thoughts of the Queen's motherly tenderness. It is a great historical event though I don't suppose it will much influence imperial policy.

> *Victoria was 81 so Dickinson had known no other monarch. She was 25 when he was born and had been on the throne nearly seven years.*

Wednesday, January 23. Shop blinds down in Otley in respect for memory of our good Queen. Her death is all the talk and the newspapers are full of particulars.

Saturday, February 2. Proclamation of King Edward VII. Watched procession of civic officials from local board offices to Parish Church. Thousands lined the streets and the church would not hold all who wanted to go in. Fanny and I attended memorial service. The King was proclaimed from the hustings in front of the Mechanics Institute. Thousands attended though it was miserable weather.

Saturday, February 9. Started for Timble after dinner. Walked up to Carr Top and then George Dickinson met me with the trap. Evening concert. I acted as chairman, also recited Burns' 'Poor and Honest Soldier'. All night at Timble. I feel it colder than Otley.

Friday, March 1. Market in afternoon. The usual country folk. I mix with them as of old. Weather roughish so feels sort of glad I have not to cross the moors.

> The farmers' wives they troop away
> From farm and village on this day
> To sell their eggs as well as butter
> And on the Cross cause quite a flutter
> They drive their bargains very mean
> And take you in if you are green

Tuesday, March 19. Up by 7. Took 9.18 train to Guiseley, called to see Mr Chippendale, architect, then walked on to Menston. Plate of hotpot at Fox and Hounds Inn, price threepence and very tasty. Then up to Menston to inspect building.

Friday, March 22. Attended Plans Committee. All passed off well. Plans for five houses to submit. I hear that the Rural Council has raised my salary from £25 to £35, so that is not so bad.

Saturday, March 23. At workhouse in forenoon, then wife and Dorothy and I started for Timble. I had to attend Parish Meeting. All business got done. Spent all night in old room at George Archer's and sister Mary Ann's.

Monday, March 25. Started for Weston to attend funeral of Joseph Dibbs of Snowden. Poor Joe had a chequered career. A man of athletic activity in youth. He married a daughter of my uncle Charles Dickinson of Swinsty, Martha, and she bore him about a dozen children. The boys have turned out bad and no help to their parents, so Joe has been handicapped and the wolf has been at his heels.

The wind is north and biting keen
A colder time was never seen
In fact it is a dreadful time
And also for my slipshod rhyme

Fanny and I are rather gloomy
The house is not sufficient roomy
Besides its far away from Timble
Also I'm old and not so nimble

Saturday, April 27. The mason business seems to be coming to an end. We are no longer in a position to run it with success. My cousin William is done for physically and I fear is the same financially, though he had his chance and should have saved money. My nephew John Archer has also failed to show true grit and I am too old now for seeing to things.

Monday, May 27. Whit Monday and Bank Holiday. Watched procession of teachers and scholars of the various Sunday Schools in the town. Great crowd in the streets.

Saturday, June 1. At 9 punctual joined William Walker and Sons employees' wagonette party on a visit to Knaresborough. Five vehicles started and 101 persons went. Dinner and tea and ticket for all the sights were provided free. The occasion was the coming of age of the newspaper, the *Wharfedale and Airedale Observer*. I was invited as a reporter. Home by 11.

Friday, June 7. Market in afternoon. Butter very low in price, only one shilling per roll of 24 ounces. Too low to pay the farmer. Eggs selling better, about 14 for a shilling.

Monday, June 10. At Huby. Cousin William very ill. We are trying to close accounts as it is desirable to get things settled before he gets too weak to attend to any business. It is already too much for him to talk for long . . .

Friday, June 21. In town in afternoon collecting rates. Got part whisky today and was latish getting home. Fanny crabbed about it and we had a little tiff. Such is married life, but I don't blame her for these wifely checks on excesses.

Monday, July 1. Drove over to Weeton house to look at some mason work. Called to see cousin William who is fast getting worse and cannot last much longer. Wife and four small children and money scarce.

Sunday, July 14. Fanny and Dorothy at Timble. I walked up Clifton Fields joining East Wood. Many walking out, lovers and others. The old old story being told over and over again. It was an evening favourable for this theme and they went at it tooth and nail.

Friday, July 19. Attended sale of two farms at White Horse, one of them the old Newsomes Farm, Shaw Hall, about 34 acres. Sold for £1,660. Another at Widra, Fewston, sold for £1,225, both very good prices I think.

Monday, July 22. Took train to Weeton. Cousin William gets weaker. The end is not far off, although he talks calm and rational about ordinary business affairs, but the frame is worn out.

Wednesday, July 24. Attended meeting of building committee of Menston Isolation Hospital at Union offices. All passed favourable for me. But George Archer arrived from Huby and reported the death of William Dickinson. This ends another close connection of my life. We were very different in thought and manner, yet we understood one another and could always work in harmony. He had a shrewd wit and could hit the mark in a dry way. He was brought up at his father's farm and began labouring for me at mason work, then contracted for the walling work at the waterworks at Fewston, Skipton and Eccup. Then in Australia for about 12 months. That was an utter failure. When he came home he and I joined in mason work and the business grew with large contracts, too large. We got too much in hand and profits latterly were partly swamped. His household expenses were heavy and I fear he has died a poor man. So the scene closes for poor Bill. He has left his mark in good solid mason work.

Sunday, August 11. Up betimes. Drove over to Timble. Fanny and Dorothy there, and we remained all night. The village is bright and sweet. Walked round fields by well-remembered nooks. A great calm and quiet seems to rest around in contrast to the noisy town of Otley.

Monday, September 9. Still alone. Fanny and Dorothy at Timble since last Friday. I feel to be getting an old man, hair turning grey. Still I suppose I look young for my years.

> Sad and alone I sit in the gloaming
> Over the past my fancy is roaming
> Life is a dream, a shadow, a fraud
> Unless we have faith in Jesus our Lord

Tuesday, September 17. Drove over to East End and Timble. A wettish day, but the hills were picturesque, the air bracing and the drive was long. The reservoirs are almost empty, and the water supply to many places is becoming a serious matter.

> Over the hills and far away
> Driving along the whole of the day
> Up hill, down dale, a merry trot
> I keep it up from spot to spot

Thursday, September 19. Up by 7 after fairly good night's rest. Kindled fire and cleaned shoes. Fanny and Dorothy got up half an hour later. Breakfast. Coffee, boiled ham shank, clap cake and short cake — these are Timble terms for pastry and a cake made of oatmeal and lard. About 5 o'clock Aunt Mary arrived with some mushrooms and we had them to tea and enjoyed them.

> Thus the days all pass away
> Thus it is we make our way
> Sometimes its smooth and ripples on
> Sometimes its rough and all goes wrong
> The years slip by, our youth is past
> We shrink before the aging blast
> The end is coming, grant that we
> May live in Paradise with Thee

Monday, September 23. Trip to Nidderdale Rant. Took train about 11 on cheap trip to Pateley Bridge. Wait at Arthington and arrived Pateley about 1 o'clock. Dinner, then walk around the picturesque town. Went to both old and new churches but did not go into agricultural show field. It came on wet and mucky. Fanny and Dorothy with me. Town crowded. A quaint interesting variety of life.

A local poet wrote of the Nidderdale Rant:

O'er t'hills an' moors
They cem in scoors
Girt skelpin' lads and lassies
An' cats an' dogs an' coos, an' Hogs
An 'osses, mules an' asses

Fat Sal fre t'Knott
Scarce gat to t'spot
Afore she lost her bustle
Which sad mishap
Quite spoilt her shap'
An' made her 'itch an' 'ustle

Saturday, September 28. Drove over to Norwood, East End House and Timble. I found things very unsatisfactory at East End. The slaters were making poor work. In Otley later I saw Hartley Thornton, the slater. He was drunk and insulting. I think he is of no further good.

Sunday, September 29. Started for Timble in wagonette with Harry Procter his wife and three children and servant. Fine morning and a pleasant drive. Roast goose to dinner. Harvest Festival at Chapel. Drove home after 8.30. Left Fanny and Dorothy, so am all alone. I feel more devotional. I feel I have got over a lot of my philosophical doubts and that a simple faith is best.

Wednesday, October 9. Took train for Leeds. Went by way of Wetherby from Harrogate. A very pretty route just opened for the Leeds and Harrogate expresses.

Tuesday, October 22. Great fire in Station Road, Otley. Cousin Harry Procter's shop burned down. Also Jackson's stores and Lawson's building roof. Fire broke out about 2 a.m. Thousands visited the scene. Harry is in a depressed state. The house owned by

Timble Methodist Chapel.

me and occupied by Mr Lupton the gas manager was injured through the heat and I shall claim off the insurance company. The wreck of Jackson's and Procter's places is complete: nothing but ashes of all that was lately so showy.

Monday, October 28. Outlook bad for cousin Harry Procter. His insurance is likely to be worthless and he will be beggared by the fire. He is still young and may rise out of the ashes but it is very disheartening.

Tuesday, November 5. Fog thick as a wall and cold as snow. Youth vigorous in celebrating Guy Fawkes Day and fires and fireworks on all hands, but the show very sorry in face of the thick mist.

> These misty days are dark and drear
> And causes accidents I fear
> Some walk into canals or rivers
> Some stay at home and get the shivers

Tuesday, November 12. My birthday. I am 57. Not looking so old as that but certainly I have aged of late and begin to feel one of the elders. The rain has come at last after a drought of unprecedented length. And it rained all day. The Wharfe was in flood and about 10 p.m. some six to eight inches in depth was running down Farnley Lane. A party of Timble folks staied drinking at the Horse Shoes Inn all last night and were still on the spree today.

> Strangely, darkly we prowl along
> Doleful at times, then singing a song
> Thus the days pass, so changeful to all
> Man rises a while, then drinks for a fall

Thursday, November 14. Our folks are busy at the new house where we purpose removing. We are in hopes of much more comfort there as the rooms are much larger and the situation altogether pleasanter than here. Besides it is more satisfactory to live in your house instead of to rent. It is perhaps a bigger house than our means can warrant but we had built it and it was there. The tenant left and we were not content with this so we decided to go and we intend to remove in a few days time.

Saturday, November 16. Mrs Chas Holmes and her son John with us in the evening. John is seven or eight and pretty intelligent, but maybe a bit spoiled being the only child. So is our Dorothy who is a sort of puzzle to us all: so erratic, so exciteable with a mixture of bright intelligence and erratic foolishness.

Monday, November 25. Removed from No. 4 Newall Mount to our own house at Field Top, Weston Lane End. Three men and horse and lurry at it all day. We got most of the things removed and set up beds so that we could stay all night. The house is larger and better and the situation much sweeter and healthier.

Monday, December 2. A cloud seems to hang over almost all our connections. Harry Procter has lost all through a fire. Our connections at Timble are troubled with the mental failure of Joseph Holmes and other affairs seem anything but hopeful. Kitchen chimney does not draw very well and my wife is very bad-tempered as a consequence.

Wednesday, Christmas Day. Only ourselves, self wife and Dorothy. Roast sparerib to dinner with etceteras. Musick and singing around. A cosy day. We are surrounded with comforts but feel isolated from our friends and our hearts are back at Timble.

I cannot say it has been a good year for me. Events have marred my fortunes and hurt my pride. My cousin and partner William Dickinson died on 24 July. We had launched out into a big business in the mason line which partly through his failing health and his incompetence in looking to details led on to neglect and the work did not run to profit as it did when I was in closer touch. Besides somehow he had drifted the wrong way in his private affairs so that he died practically bankrupt and his widow has had to apply to the Guardians for relief.

1902

I spent the end of the old and the beginning of the new year at my dear old native village. Slept all night at Joseph Holmes, Chapel House, and staied to dinner and then about 2 o'clock started off and walked home to Newall. In the evening I heated the oven and stewed pigs' feet and roasted sparerib. So begins the New Year. I have banished a lot of my former unbelief.

Thursday, January 2. Very lonely in house by myself. But the cat is capital company and rubs and purrs quite coaxingly.

Monday, January 6. Up at 7. Drove off to East End, Norwood, then on to Timble where I loosed out and had dinner. About 3 o'clock started for home, Fanny with me. We left Dorothy at Timble.

Friday, January 10. Our sleeping room is airy and should be healthy. Milk carts and workmen are on the move early and we can hear them passing before it is light. Went round the town paying accounts at about ten places. Snow is threatening.

> Thus passes by the short-lived day
> And lights us on life's changeful way
> Age with the years creeps on apace
> Gray hairs are growing on my face
> May wisdom come as years increase
> And may my latter days be peace

Monday, February 16. Only a poor night and could not get warm in bed. The Wharfe still frozen over and skating in full swing. About 11 o'clock George Archer came with news that Joseph Holmes had died very suddenly about 6 o'clock this morning. The event touches us closely as Joe married my Aunt Mary, my wife's mother, and my wife and Dorothy are there at present.

Wednesday, March 26. Weather very cold and the outlook not so good either for seed time or the holidays. The war in Africa drags on and Imperial affairs are by no means rosy. But I suppose old England will once more prevail and get control as before.

Friday, March 28. Cecil Rhodes the Empire builder is dead. So is Alfred Cook of Leeds.

Tuesday, April 8. At Menston in forenoon. Walked there except for a lift part of the way on a ginger beer wagon. Rode back on a Motor Car, my first ride on one of those modern innovations. I think they will have come to stay and I predict that in a few years time they will be common on all roads.

Tuesday, April 29. Mrs John Margerrison of Timble came in the afternoon to register the death of her husband John. Poor Jack, he was a somewhat queer-tempered little fellow but we overlooked his faults and now see only what was good in him. He was only 42. Thus we pass . . . we shall be forgotten as those who once held sway in ancient Rome and other old-time places. Surely this is a world of mysteries, but we must make the best we can of it . . . I am getting more used to the new life. I don't think I should care to go back to Timble for good. Yet a great longing for the old haunts comes over me at times which I cannot control. Fanny is homesick and loves the old home.

Sunday, June 1. Walked up to Carr Top in the evening. Great commotion about 7.30 p.m. bells ringing, whistles sounding, and a great bonfire in market place. News had arrived that the Boer War was at an end. Great enthusiasm and streets crowded. Everybody rejoicing. Speech by Chairman of the Council. Much cheering.

Monday, June 2. Rejoicing and general holiday. Boys marching in troops dressed fantastically in mock military style. Up to midnight great crowds in the town. Powerful electric light in Kirkgate and music and dancing. Gloriously fine and warm. Here we are much perturbed about a little affair at Timble. A lodger at Aunt Mary's who persists in dressing in female apparel. They refuse to quit him in spite of our remonstrances.

Wednesday, June 4. The news from Timble caused me to give up a journey to Pool and along with Harry Procter and George Holmes drove over to Timble through heavy rain. A gentleman had come to Aunt Mary's as a lodger. He dressed every day as a fine lady. Remonstrance from us having failed to stop this thing we went over and insisted on his immediate removal which we saw effected. He rode off on his bicycle about 8 o'clock and we hope this is the last of a very strange affair. He said he was a clergyman from Birmingham and he seemed decent and sensible but for this strange whim. The villagers were much excited and a raid on the house was imminent.

Tuesday, June 10. Took 10 train to Ilkley. An otter hunt was going on so I followed the folks down to the Denton road. The hounds were on the scent and hundreds of people were present. I staied over an hour until the otter was killed amid much excitement.

The hounds were out in early morn
And cheery was the huntsman's horn
They found a drag in Crown Wheel Deep
But slyly did the otter creep

From place to place with stealthy speed
Till hounds and men paid little heed
Until at last downstream he went
The hounds gave music at the scent
Until the varmint ran aground
And soon was worried by a hound

Thursday, June 12. Writing out report for Plans Committee and much work about Rate collecting. We are lonely all along now. We feel cut off from Timble. Recent events have led on to extravagance. I suppose it will blow over by and by.

Cold cold the June wind blows
It feels as if it came off snows
But still the grass it grows apace
And Nature shows a smiling face

Monday, June 16. Auction mart and several county folk there. They go for a little life and drinking. Although they say farming is bad they spend freely careless of the future. Nowadays perhaps more than ever man is all for pleasure and the serious work of life does not command the same attention as formerly . . . But wealth has increased and luxury abounds amid much poverty.

Tuesday, June 24. Going into Otley I was startled to hear that the King is ill and an operation has to be performed and consequently the Coronation is postponed indefinitely. Everybody seems confounded.

Thursday, June 26. All very flat and quiet on what was to have been Coronation Day, so Fanny and Dorothy and I took the 1.49 train to Bolton Bridge and then on by conveyance to The Strid. I was never at The Strid before. The woods are beautiful the water clear as crystal and The Strid a wonderful freak of Nature.

> *The broad Wharfe pours through a channel only four to five feet wide gouged through solid rock. The narrow but deep water has tempted many to leap across, and according to legend the Boy of Egremont was drowned when his leashed hound held back as he tried to leap The Strid.*

Tuesday, July 1. Fanny and Dorothy and Lotty returned from a stay in Timble. I had been alone all night. Magic lantern entertainment by Mr John Edson in our parlour in the evening. Scenes depicted were of Paris and Brussels and the journey between. Very interesting, but I was well tired and glad our folks had come home.

Thursday, July 3. Gathering in the Rate for Newall. This is not such pleasant work among the artisan class as I have always found it among farmers. Few of the working folk seem to have anything saved up to meet an extra payment. What they will do after getting into Otley when Newall is joined to the town and having their Rate doubled I don't know. It seems like being a great strain and I should not like to have to collect the Rate then.

Friday, July 4. Market Day again. About 1*s* 3*d* per 24-ounce roll of butter and eggs 14 for a shilling. Beef much dearer than it has been. Season late and strawberries only just in. Potatoes dear being twopence per pound. Beautiful weather.

> Midsummer now is resplendent and gay
> Foliage is rich and long is the day
> Man seeking for pleasure wanders abroad
> And cycles and motors are crowding the road

Monday, July 7. Up by 7.30. We don't rise so soon. Our bedroom is airy and sweet and we like to linger there. A warm windy day. Haytime in full swing, but I am out of it now, going round Rate collecting. My time seems to be a sort of half holiday and half work.

Over in Otley and about home mainly and on registration or plans work. The duties are light and easy, but I am getting on in life and it is quite as much as I care for . . . Julia Saunders from Clifton is come to help Fanny wash. These washing days have to be faced.

Friday, July 18. I am growing side whiskers again after having for the past year or two shaved off all except the upper lip. I think the hair gives strength to muscles, especially if you have been used to it.

Wednesday, July 30. Mrs Hunter came looking at our old oak furniture. She bid £5 for our long settle — a good price but we feel as if we don't want to part with any of our old oak things.

Saturday, August 9. Church bells ringing merrily by 6 a.m. for the coronation of King Edward the Seventh. Over in Otley all busy giving finishing touches to decorations. Service at the parish church at 11, band in Market Place at 2 p.m. and later in cricket field where coronation fêtes were going off. Torchlight procession in the evening and loyal salute of rockets from parish church.

Thursday, September 2. In the early hours of the morning Fanny was taken ill and the result was a miscarriage. We had not expected this although she had been unwell for the past month or two. Sent Walter Roundell for Lotty Holmes to Timble and all went favourable.

Wednesday, September 24. Fanny and I walked up to Clifton and got a few hazel nuts. It was a warm fine day. Fanny is only weakly yet, but I think she is gaining strength. I don't think she is of really strong physique though she is a big heavy fresh-looking woman, perhaps a stone heavier than I am. Dorothy is only a delicate little girl, but I have faith she will improve both in her mind and body after a year or two.

Thursday, September 25. Making a final effort to get the Rate in. It is slow work with some of them. At White Horse a bit in afternoon . . . We get our using water from a spring near the weir to Garnett's mill. It is capital water.

Monday, October 1. Walked to Leathley. Sale there for Mrs Teale. I bought an old oak settle for £2 12*s*. There is always good competition for these old oak things.

Thursday, October 2. Met Mr Dodgson and paid him £85 for a plot of building ground next to our house.

Wednesday, October 8. Walter Roundell drove me to Castly and then Huby. I bought a horse and trap of Mrs Mundell for Aunt Mary.

Saturday, October 11. Town and around. Aunt Mary and Dorothy came about noon in the new turnout, viz. old horse, old trap but newish gear. All cost me £12 15*s*. A very good combination and it answers well.

Monday, October 20. Very wet dirty day. At auction mart looking after cattle put in by Aunt Mary from Timble. Price not really satisfactory, but no remedy. These auction marts are vile places. A company of unprincipled jobbers are all ready to connive in any move to cheat or pervert a fair course of business.

Friday, October 31. Sam Holmes and Bob Spence, two Timble young men, up for breaking windows at Mrs Newall's, at Snowden Bank Bottom. A most dastardly act. Old Mary Newall being just turned 89 years old and her son Andrew 60. This is a sad commentary on our School Board education and on the influence of the Free Library at Timble.

Saturday, November 8. Fanny and Dorothy off to Timble. I started in Walter Walker's trap to Norwood to measure slating. Then on by Timble and staied there all night. Attended Club meeting, a revival of the old life. Fanny looks careworn and ill and Dorothy is only a puny girl. So there we are.

Tuesday, November 11. Down at Pool looking at buildings and drains. Our family are not really in good health all along and life is not so enjoyable as it was in the sunny days of youth. Yet in those days the blessings were not appreciated and we invented imaginary troubles. Such is this strange life. The puzzle is what it is all about. Will the veil ever be lifted?

Wednesday, November 12. This is my 58th birthday. Home in forenoon writing, then took 1.8 train to Ilkley and walked across to Middleton and inspected drain at Mr Sallet's house up in the woods. Walked back on the old road to Denton and through the park to Askwith. Met Mr Boothman there and had tea at his house. Staied about an hour then walked on to Weston and rode home with Albany Holmes's son who delivers milk at our house. Home in the evening, pretty well tired.

Thursday, November 13. Up late at 8.30. Julia Saunders at the door having come to help Fanny to clean down a little. Over in town myself and took pieces for the Otley paper. I think I must buckle on my literary armour and write more for the paper. I used to have the talent for touching up popular questions with a rather fine edge of wit and sarcasm. Sometimes it made enemies but upon the whole it added to my reputation.

Thursday, November 20. I kindled the fire and partly prepared breakfast before Fanny and Dorothy came down. Dorothy is a whining sort of a child as yet and I don't think she is so forward or well developed physically or mentally as most girls of her age. I sometimes fear that the fact of Fanny and I being cousins may account for her weakness. At some things she is very quick and bright, but she is so variable. I confess I am unable to judge what is in her.

Tuesday, November 25. Fanny and Dorothy back from Timble yesterday and today I was at Menston and had tea with my old housekeeper now Mrs Wilkinson, formerly Alice Spence. Walked there and back.

Walking and talking from day to day
So we pass along our way
In time the mists will roll away
And we shall hail a brighter day
The Spring will come bedecked with flowers
And birds will sing in leafy bowers.

Friday, December 12. To Court House to get Rate signed. Staied in court hearing a bastardy case in which a girl of 16 sued a married man. The case was of a very blue character and was dismissed.

Thursday, December 25. Christmas Day and a very high wind but mild temperature. Aunt Mary and Lotty arrived about 12. Roast goose to dinner. In the afternoon a terrible gale sprang up so that it was dangerous driving. At Harry Procter's shop it blew a large hoarding down and stripped off part of the roof sheets. About 3.30 Lotty and Dorothy started in the trap for Timble. The wind was terrific. Dorothy's hat which was in a paper bag behind the trap fell out and was carried away over the meadows where I found it later on. How they got home I don't know. Aunt Mary here all night and anxious as to whether Lotty and Dorothy got to Timble safely.

Wednesday, December 31. At 1 o'clock Fanny and I started off for Timble. Polly Holmes met us with trap at Clifton Lane End and we had a pleasant drive over the moors. The annual supper for the inhabitants and all who come took place in the Library. The attendance was very large. Dancing up to 2 a.m. It was the old ways over again. No programme and consequently no order or discipline. The young folk seemed to enjoy themselves and the elders looked on pleased with the scene. Just after 11 I wished all a happy and prosperous New Year on behalf of the Trustees. At Timble all night.

As the old year closed the stars shone with unusual brightness from the clear blue vault over Timble filling the minds of those who looked and thought with wonder at the magnificence and mystery of Creation . . . I don't think there is much difference in the burden of cares we have each to bear. The rich find them on the higher platform of life as well as the poor on the lower.

The past year has been fairly successful for me from a business point of view. I am not just satisfied to live in this house. It is too big and absorbs too much of our capital . . . I am still very erect and active on foot but it requires a strong effort of philosophy to shake off a feeling of depression at times. But I am not one who cannot submit to the inevitable. I try to forget the past and pledge myself to do my best in the future . . . I feel that one cannot do anything better than peg away at the nearest duty.

1907

Dickinson gives no indication that at the end of 1902 he ceased to keep a diary for the next five years. But the pattern of his life has changed very little. Dorothy is nearly 16 and still a puzzle and a problem . . . widowed Aunt Mary comes to live with her daughter . . .

Tuesday, January 1. Here we are again, well and hearty considering our years. I was up betimes as old Pepys would say but to miserable weather. A thaw is in progress. The roads are all slush and showers prevail . . . Our folks are washing. Julia Saunders here to help. I have been busy all day making out returns for registrations of births and deaths and vaccinations. I stuck close to the work and feel as if I have opened the year industriously. Dorothy at Timble. Am teetotal today and feels very abstemious in every sense. The Workhouse Infirmary opened today.

Thursday, January 3. I am a bit depressed, probably through my old enemy dyspepsia, which I think is chronic with me.

> But what care I? We all must die
> From one cause or another
> So why repine and mope and sigh
> We must return to earth, our mother

Friday, January 4. J. Archer and Aunt Betty and cousin Patty Dickinson here to dinner. They do pour in for a cheap feed from Allerton way.

Tuesday, January 8. Registered two deaths and made about 13 shillings from fees for certificates. This source of my income brings in a nice sum. I trust that by economising I may do well financially this year if health and other things favour. Fanny and Aunt Mary at our neighbours the Woods. They are more friendly disposed than when we came here at first.

Friday, January 11. Registered death of John Myers of Fewston. Poor Johnny. A man of one talent, but changing from being a wild young man he turned religious and teetotal and became well off and respected. He lived alone and was found dead in bed.

Tuesday, January 15. Writing out my monthly report as Buildings Surveyor. Evening at Mr John King's to supper. A pleasant time up to 11 p.m. A gramophone gave songs. Very interesting.

Monday, January 21. Much concern now publicly on account of Dr Campbell's New Theology. These theologies are a subject of contention in all ages. Is it man's utter inability to see through the great mystery of life and death which causes all this stir?

Thursday, January 24. Cousin Thomas Dickinson up from 2 to 5. Tom has some strange ideas on the Millenial Dawn which he feels sure will commence in about eight years.

We come and go both to and fro
We meet a friend with 'How d'you do?'
We call and have a glass or so
And then to other business go
And so from childhood days we pass
And hardly know what is or was

Tuesday, February 5. A meeting tonight in the Robinson Library at Timble to protest against this new school arrangement.

Wednesday, February 6. Writing out petition to have the school arrangements altered at Timble. This is a burning question in the village and district.

What bother there is in running affairs
Likewise the same in running in pairs
Be they horses or asses or women or men
In fact I find bother in running missen

Friday, February 8. Miserably cold so came home from town and stuck close to the fire which we keep pretty well piled with fuel. How wondrous are the provisions which our Creator has made for his children on this earth. Amongst the first may be counted coal of which the supply is practically inexhaustible. Other products of almost equal importance follow, all showing that there must have been foresight in all this and that only a good and all-seeing Power could have planned this marvellous scheme.

We are all very busy one way and another
Fanny storms at her daughter, at me and her mother
But when cleaning gets done and all looks pretty bright
We sit cosy and happy till late in the night.

Wednesday, February 13. Attended sale of effects of the late Henry Newstead at his residence in Borogate. I bought three pictures for 1*s* 3*s*. One is the Lord's Prayer executed in 1858 by C. Tunnicliffe of Burley. I think it is a bargain. I also bought three walking sticks for 1*s* 2*d*.

These market days come regular
The people come from·near and far
From Brumley Head and Dacre Banks
They come in traps or tramp on shanks
But walking now is not the vogue
None walks but vagabond or rogue

Thursday, February 21. Visited almost every house in Clifton and intermediate houses collecting the Rate. Got a good lot in. Home about 8 p.m. Letter from H. Procter telling of severe weather at Lethbridge in southern Alberta where they are now living.

The wind nips keen, the roads are hard
It don't agree with this poor bard

Friday, February 22. Meeting of Library Trustees to consider the action of the caretaker, John Ward, who locked the door on a social gathering on Saturday last. It was decided to dismiss John at once. I have had much trouble about this Library from the inception. What letters I have written to the donor, Mr Gill, and what work I have done for nothing. Still we must strive whilst we are here.

At home I've been most of the day
That's where I'm most inclined to stay
As years creep on and youth recedes
A corner chair supplies my needs

Tuesday, March 5. Up at 7.30. Washed and shaved. Breakfast coffee and bacon. Then the morning paper and other little items of business. We take the *Leeds Mercury* and the *Yorkshire Evening*

Post, both only a halfpenny each. We also get *The Wharfedale Observer* free because I report for it, and a given-away sheet published by Chas. Walker in Otley, so we get many papers at a small cost.

Wednesday, March 13. At Pool Bank in afternoon re plans of house for B. Whitaker and Sons. Caught in storm of sleet and rain coming back. It faced me plumb in front so I got wet through. I have not had such a wetting for many years so I am very careful on that point fearing rheumatic fever which I have had before. Stripped and changed. A dressmaker at our house, little and young but they say she frames very well.

Saturday, March 16. Wild and wet and the Wharfe flooded. Dinner of roast mutton. Cousin Thomas Dickinson here an hour or two. He had been over at Isaac Ingleby's near Huddersfield hedging. Isaac married cousin Patty Dickinson and they have taken a farm over there.

The storms may rage all round the spot
We find safe shelter in our cot
The seas may roar the waves may roll
The mountain storms may screech and howl
We care not if the Welkin rocks
If our good Castle stands its shocks
At times like this our thoughts will flee
To Him who calmed Lake Galilee

Tuesday, March 19. Still wild and windy. Various business in forenoon.

The wind it blows, the poor old crows
Are having stormy times
Old Nature strikes with heavy blows
While fools are making rhymes

Wednesday, March 20. Weather somewhat calmer but still blowing half a gale. Up to Clifton and got all the Rate in. So another half years overseer's work is got through.

They say a calm comes after storm
If not the weather's not in form
They say that pain comes after pleasure
But after labour well-earned leisure

Saturday, April 6. Tea at David Boothman's. Arranged to make will for Mrs Boothman's mother. Home about 7.30. A young woman waiting to have a birth registered. A very good-looking young woman who had fallen away from virtuous ways. More the pity of it.

Saturday, April 20. Planted 20 red cabbages first thing. About home till 2 p.m. then to Clifton Parish Council meeting. I am clerk but only three were present. Cold rain fell on my journey home and felt very miserable, maybe dyspepsia the cause.

> Sorrow and trouble are the common lot of all
> Dogging man and woman ever since the Fall
> The orthodox, so faithful, would have us all believe
> That all our toil and trouble are due to Mother Eve

Monday, April 29. Miserable weather but our folks are happily getting nearly over with the cleaning terror. Oh, how happy we hope to be then. Our Dorothy is getting to be a big strong girl and should be useful to her mother, but I fear that Fanny does not possess the gift to train her in the best fashion as she is too hot in her temper and begets retaliation instead of obedience. I trust that common sense will prevail. Weather cold and showery and I have a bit of rheumatic twitching.

> Rheumatic pains with grips and strains
> Beset as Time upon us gains
> The days of youth will ne'er come more
> I'm nearly three besides three score

Saturday, May 4. Second day of Otley Show. Wind stronger and colder than yesterday when a large tent was blown down. Tents blown down again today. I went into town in the evening and had some whisky.

Wednesday, May 8. Over in town and wrote article for Otley paper on coming visit of the Rev. Robt. Collyer. In garden almost all rest of day. Stomach out of order. Oatmeal porridge to supper last night. Took one of Cockles Pills this evening. It may relieve me somewhat. The night air cuts very keen.

Saturday, May 11. Fanny and Dorothy went to Leeds by the 9.14

train to buy finery. They came back soon after 6 with news of Leeds and the stirring life and wealth there. Fine things in fine shops in Briggate and Boar Lane and music and dinner at the Ceylon Cafe.

Thursday, May 16. Up at 8 and mowing the lawn and tidying up for the holidays. Few — though I say it — can do better than myself in the way of making things look tidy and orderly.

Saturday, May 18. We have all our gardens and lawns in prim order and fit for Whitsuntide. The house inside is bright and clean and we ought to feel comfortable and content, but how near we come to ideal content I cannot say. Perhaps we are past the prime to enjoy life as we used to do, but we live well and enjoy average health. So what more do we want? I pulled some gooseberries today and had gooseberry pasty and new milk to supper.

Whit Monday, May 20. Cold with showers. The Bradford 40-mile walkers passing from one o'clock to three. What a foolish thing it seems of these men to strain themselves to this extent. Parade of school children. Thousands on the streets and the town very lively.

Tuesday, May 21. Up at 7. W. Roundell came with a small wagonette at 9.30 and we all drove off to Timble. There was a bitterly cold north wind and it rained most of the journey. There was a poor muster for the Club Walk. Dinner was served in the large room at the village inn. A meeting was held to consider the position of the Lodge and a halfpenny per week was put on the contributions. This Club anniversary is simply a debauch of eating and drinking and speaks but poorly for fallen humanity.

Wednesday, May 22. Up at 7.30. Town in forenoon and then took 1.6 train to Arthington and walked over Arthington Banks to Five Lane Ends at Adel to inspect a house. Walked back to Pool station and took 5.26 train home. Very pleasant walk through Creskeld Fields and wood. I never heard such a grand and varied orchestral chorus of birdsong. It was simply marvellous, so hilarious seemed the thousand throats . . . I was well tired with the ten miles of walking.

Sunday, May 26. Fine growing weather. We had roast beef and new potatoes for the first time this season. Fanny at chapel in the morning, Dorothy at Clifton Chapel in the afternoon. A wet evening. Fanny and Aunt Mary at the Mission Room to hear Old Mo. Dorothy in house reading *Barnaby Rudge.* We had oatmeal porridge to supper.

Wednesday, June 5. Rain falling in torrents and land like a sea. Thomas Dickinson here talking on the problems of religion.

Poor Tom he once was young and tall and strong
He loved the girls, he liked his beer and didn't think it wrong
The years rolled on and Tom grew old and sere
And Tom turned good and gave up girls and beer

Monday, July 1. Busy most of the day making out quarterly and monthly returns as Registrar, Assistant Overseer, and Vaccination Officer. I bought Cassell's *History of England*, eight volumes, for six shillings and we pore in it with interest.

Monday, July 8. Up about 7. Kindled fire and cut some ham and fried it for breakfast. A very cold morning. Dorothy's birthday. She is 16 today. She goes up to Clifton on Monday evenings to practice music on the piano with Miss Gillard.

Wednesday, July 10. Fanny and I took the 1.4 train to Leeds. A little income tax business there after which we took a tram to Roundhay Park. But a thunder storm came on and all was deluged. Took tram back and then patronised the first performance at the Empire Music Hall. Had supper at a restaurant and home by the 10.10 train. We bought Dorothy a silver watch, price £1 9*s* with clasp. We also spent freely other ways but we only go out once in a while.

Friday, July 12. All the ordinary market folk in evidence, but the market is not what it used to be for the farmers. Foreign produce comes in with such keen competition that home produce is playing only a secondary role in most things, butter especially, which ought to be still the first if only the farmers would combine and make good stuff. But they don't and so here they are stranded and poor.

Of strawberries, rasps, and cherries and stuff
The market seems glutted with more than enough
From all the world over supplies coming here
Which makes the home farmer grumble and swear

Tuesday, July 16. George and I drove to Blubberhouses to look at old buildings at the late Frankland Arms, with a view to using them for new cemetery chapel in Meagill Lane.

> *John Dickinson lies buried in the new cemetery, Fanny and his sister Mary Ann beside him.*

Wednesday, July 17. George Archer here re the estimates for the new cemetery chapel at Meagill Lane, Fewston. A most glorious day. Moderate health but not robust.

Tuesday, July 23. Went to Mudds, dentist, to have teeth fitted. At 7.30 Fanny and I attended Mechanics Institute where General Booth, founder of the Salvation Army addressed a crowded meeting, enthusiastic and in every way successful.

Sunday, July 28. Very fine summer-like day. Mutton chops and green peas to dinner. Dorothy, Fanny and I walked to Snowden and attended a camp meeting at Crag. Many present, chiefly young women and girls. Tea at Eli Dale's, also supper. Pleasant walk home.

Monday, July 29. Writing report of Snowden service for Otley paper. I think I have made a good report with philosophised reasonings in it. The brick house has just got the first floor on and they are stopping our view from the kitchen.

Wednesday, July 31. Up betimes. A fine morning. In moderate health. Some progress made with the hay, but then showers came. The Test cricket match at Headingley, between England and South Africa concluded today. England won. Well done, old England.

Tuesday, August 6. Fanny, Dorothy and Aunt Mary took the 12.40 train to Harrogate to see the gay life there. I took the 3.32 to Ilkley and inspected house building on the Middleton estate. Then I walked up on the moor and took the road towards Keighley and persevered onward and upward. Up and up, the air purer and I believe I struck the ozone. Still I persevered to gratify an old wish until I could see into Airedale. The scenery was glorious. I had a field glass which helped me to locate places. Then I trotted down to Ilkley and took the 8.40 train home. Our women arrived at the same time, so supper and to bed.

Monday, August 12. Fanny went to stay at Timble. Dorothy and I alone. Dorothy makes herself useful but requires pushing to get any work out of her.

Stomach out of order, spirits rather down
I didn't get much comfort passing through the town.
The stinks and smells in Bay Horse Yard
Would poison any decent bard
The blood and rags in the New Cross
Are bad enough to kill a hoss

Sunday, August 18. It is 32 years today since my father died and I am now about the age he was when he died.

Tuesday, August 20. Fanny bought a malt loaf for tea and I enjoyed it heartily and felt quite fresh and strong after so commenced and mew the lawn. At it till dusk, then read the evening paper and boiled milk and bread with a nice drop of whisky in it to supper.

Friday, August 23. Went up to station to meet Dr Collyer and his niece Miss Roberts. Hearty greetings. I had acquainted several of the leading people of the town of Dr Collyer's visit and there was quite a reception in the market place. Dr Collyer came to our house to dinner and staied to tea. He is still bright and genial as ever and has an inexhaustible fund of anecdote. To think that he was once a poor boy at Blubberhouse factory working over 70 hours a week.

Wednesday, September 4. Up, shaved and dressed and at station at 9.50. Mr Hunter took me over in his motor car. Then Dr Collyer, the Rev. S. Parkinson myself and Mr Hunter with chauffeur started for Bolton Bridge and thence to Blubberhouses. Called at Scaife Hall and Hopper Lane to luncheon. Then by way of Fewston to Timble and called to see Uncle George and the Library. Then down to Harrogate. Put up at the Grosvenor Hotel. Mr Parkinson, Dr Collyer and myself staied all night. Had good entertainment. Dr Collyer held up well for his years. He is 84, but felt tired towards night . . . Motoring is good for getting to places but hardly so pleasant and leisurely travelling as by carriage and horse. The two poets of the Washburn valley, Mr Collyer and Mr Parkinson and myself comprised most of the literary talent now left belonging to the Washburn valley.

Thursday, September 5. Only moderate sleep. Walked up Valley Gardens and to Pump Room before breakfast, in company with a sea captain. Dr Collyer not in very good order and the morning being wet the proposed visit to Knaresborough was abandoned. Dr Collyer took tickets, he for Leeds and I for Otley by the 10.30 train.

Friday, September 20. Market place pretty full but public houses almost deserted where years ago they used to be full. What does it mean? Are people becoming more sober? Now I also notice that teetotal beverages are more drunk than they used to be. Let us hope that more sober times are coming.

Pains within and pains without
Just what I ail I can't find out
My flesh is weak my spirits flat
I am antipodes to fat

Wednesday, October 2. Hurried to catch the 1.49 train to Ilkley, Fanny and Dorothy with me. Just in time for the meeting at the new Town Hall. Mr Benson a councillor, reserved us a good seat at the front and we heard Dr Collyer's address and other speeches. Bade adieu to Dr Collyer who rode off triumphant amid cheers of the multitude. He seems beloved and honoured by all who come in contact with him . . . We feel a tender love for the old man . . . We shall never see his like again.

Wednesday, October 9. Up at 7.30. The women came down later in order — Fanny, Dorothy and then Aunt Mary. So we sat down to breakfast, toast and butter. I had done the toast so we had a fairly good breakfast with coffee and cheese. Then I went over to Otley on shopping errands while the women were ironing and starching. Dinner was bacon and potatoes and pancakes. Then I was at Mudds getting a few teeth altered. Porridge to supper.

Thursday, November 14. Over in town with cabbages to pickle. Writing most of the day and inclined for the corner chair. Old Joe Spence, the sailor of Timble, used to tell of an old man at Fenton who said that the world was too small for a young man but a corner chair was sufficient for an old man. I begin to feel the truth of it.

Wednesday, November 27. Had pigs liver fry to dinner. Fanny and Dorothy cleaning for Christmas. I had bought two fat pigs from George Holmes for £12 10*s*. Rendered pigs migerum (belly fat for lard) today. Fanny and Dorothy busy cleaning and baking.

The days are dark and dull
Our women push and pull
At cleaning up and all about
No rest inside so I go out

Sunday, December 8. Pork pie and coffee to breakfast and roast shank to dinner. Very rough wild wet day. Fanny and Dorothy at chapel but I was never out.

Thursday, December 19. Hung flitches and hams of the fat pig we salted three weeks since. Robert Dawson our neighbour who lived at the farm a little further up the road was buried today. His brothers John and Joseph both bachelors are left to carry on the farm. They are perhaps the oldest family of farmers in Wharfedale.

Wednesday, Christmas Day. Up — was it 9 did they say? The goose was the thing, 10½lbs for 9*s* 2*d* or close on 11*d* per lb bought of Mrs Walker of Park Farm, Denton, and had to be cooked. It was cooked, juicy, savoury and altogether good. I took a walk up to Clifton and came back with an appetite, so we all four sat down, Aunt Mary, Fanny and Dorothy and myself. Savoury pudding first, then the goose and etceteras after. A little walk before tea. Band of music playing around. A few boys and girls calling for Christmas gifts. Cold east wind but fair and no frost. I sent a quantity of cards with photo of Robert Collyer on by post. One should be thankful for the many comforts we enjoy, food and fire in abundance. What more can we want?

Thursday, December 26. Cold wind. Two little girls came singing simple pieces. They looked poor and cold so we called them in and gave them food and coppers and they warmed their hands and went away rejoicing.

Monday, December 30. Snow on the hills. Joe Bolton arrested.

The year 1907 has not used me and my immediate connections very badly all the time. We have had fairly good health. Our business and social life has been fairly successful. I don't seek public place or position in Otley but I see that if I wanted to come forward I could soon fill a niche in the town's temple of honour. Fanny takes a part in connection with the Wesleyan Chapel and gets put to the front abundantly. Dorothy is now grown almost a woman of fairly good looks and of physical build much stouter and taller than we used to think she would ever attain. My Aunt Mary, Fanny's mother, lives with us and we each have our daily tasks and duties. My life seems to be more and more in the past and a younger generation has sprung up with which I cannot keep in touch. I have learned however to look on the turmoil and straining bustle of life with much less anxiety and am content if I can attend to my ordinary duties and just keep the financial balance on the right side. Of course I have still some smouldering embers of the old ambition left in my nature and hopes of brighter days and better luck to come if I am spared to work a little longer. And if not, why then I am ready to resign and submit to the inevitable laws of Nature. We still live in this big house worth a rent of £30 a year and our expenses are consequently bigger than they ought to be. I find that with all our expenses I have a balance of about £20 to the good during 1907.

1908

We now enter upon another year . . . I have made no resolutions and so shall not have the trouble of breaking them. I may try to mend a bit in some of my ways and manners but I don't look for much being done . . . The future is an enigma and we all have hopes that a good thing or two may fall in our way. May it be so for me and mine . . .

Wednesday, January 1. I rose about 8 and kindled the fire. It had frozen a bit in the night and the Chevin has a thin coating of snow. I took the 1.4 train to Pool for my registration station, but no business turned up. The birth rate seems to be declining.

Saturday, January 4. After dinner started for Timble, frost keen and the roads clean and dry. Scores skating on the Tewit Pond at Carr Top. Tea at sister Ann's. Collecting Rate during the evening and tasting cheese and glasses of whisky. Staied all night at sister's and slept with nephew George Archer.

Monday, January 6. Fanny and Dorothy at Timble all night and Aunt Mary and I alone in the house. Slept badly. Couldn't get warm. The Wharfe came down in flood and skating quite knocked out.

> Change in the weather, change in all things
> Customs and manners and old forms take wings
> They fly out of use and never return
> But yet to make butter you still have to churn

Saturday, January 11. Went into town to buy some postcards. The market place was fairly busy. A quack doctor was holding forth most wonderful stories of cures for all diseases. Weather very severe but right enough for mid-winter.

Thursday, January 16. Drove to Timble where I delivered notice to Mrs Fortune at Chapel House re an order for her ejectment.

Friday, January 24. At court to get order for ejecting Maria Fortune from Chapel House at Timble. She has been a poor tenant in every sense and we want to get rid of her as we have let the house to Thomas Pearson of High Snowden who will be a much better tenant. Such are the little battles we have to fight, but we cannot get through life without these troubles.

Sunday, January 26. Up at 9. Washed and dressed. Roast rabbit to dinner. Very wild wet day and the mist has lifted. Dorothy and I at Wesleyan Chapel in evening. Preacher very orthodox in the old order.

> The mists they come and stay awhile
> And genders in me angry bile
> The winds then come and clear the air
> And Nature's face once more is fair

Wednesday, February 12. Took 1 p.m. train to Guiseley. Walked to Esholt Hall to see engineers preparing the Bradford sewerage scheme. The Hall with its once beautiful surroundings is now the centre of the scheme, and the once sylvan scene is spoiled by the conglomeration of population and the sparkling waters are now inky black. Such is the march of progress. I marched up Esholt Spring to Guiseley took the train to Menston and walked home, well tired as a man of 63 might well be.

Tuesday, February 25. My female staff, viz Fanny, Dorothy and Aunt Mary are rather bad getters-up. And this was washing day, so I kindled the fire and lit the set pot and filled it. Then they arose in their might and attacked the washing and also baking, so they did very well. I began dressing stone for a wall I am going to build and I tired myself well not being used to this work lately.

Tuesday, March 3. Fanny and Dorothy took train to Bramhope and will stay all night at Pennington's. Aunt Mary had already gone there for an indefinite stay, so I am left alone. In house all evening reading Dickens' *Dombey and Son.* What a master of humour and pathos was this Dickens, and how vivid and life-like his characters.

Wednesday, March 4. Took 1.6 train to Pool, registered birth there then 3.26 train back. Fanny and Dorothy met me at Pool station and came home with me. Cold day. Snow falling. Registered a death on arrival home and gave six certificates at 2*s* 7*d* each. Made

16 shillings today out of birth and death certificates. If every day brought this amount things would boom. The weather is very trying and much sickness prevails and many old people are dropping off.

One by one Death claims his dues
And unconcerned we hear the news
O may we learn from others' fate
To live meet for a future state

Wednesday, March 18. Joe Bolton's sentence is twelve months in the second degree. Well, it looks very light for his crimes and Otley is angry about it.

Cold and keen the March winds blow
Most likely we shall have more snow

Saturday, April 4. Voted for Urban District Councillors about 11 a.m. Myers and Cobley got in. I went over about 10 p.m. to hear the poll results, but it rained so I adjourned to the Liberal Club. Part excitement going off. The town is roused against Joe Bolton and the sympathisers in his villany. Removing stones and things at back. I am making desperate efforts to get things sided.

Hard work is the common lot of man
He has to do as he will and can
But when the strength of youth is on the wane
His toil is mixed with gripping aches and pain
So to be brief and just to save dissensions
I advocate immediate old age pensions

Friday, April 17. A fine sunny day but a cold north-east wind. Many people passing and repassing our house on their Good Friday holiday. We have much work on hand just now. Forenoon in garden siding up, afternoon writing certificate copies, and the women at it all day cleaning down. For my part the bustle of these holiday times has no attraction. I prefer a quiet walk in a country lane where the birds are singing and flowers grow. And oh for a bird's nest to remind me of my rough rude life as a boy.

Thursday, April 23. Snow showers and winterly. Making out Rate in afternoon. This work entails a lot of bother as I have to make out new Rates at 2*s* 3*d* in the pound and it is bad to work out correctly.

Friday, April 24. Much talk about the death of William Smithson, insurance agent of Burley and formerly of Timble, a contemporary of mine as a young man. Always a nice civil fellow, but a few years ago his wife died and he was subject to fits of depression. At last he went down to the Wharfe and drowned himself.

Wednesday, April 29. Fanny and Dorothy at Leeds and spent about £4 on dress and other items. Money goes fast, faster than it comes.

Saturday, May 2. Up at 7. Our women all in uproar with this terrible cleaning down business. I washed and dressed and started off for Timble. Called at the Roebuck and had a glass of beer and twopennyworth of cheese and bread and rose refreshed. Called at Herbert Procter's at Snowden and had dandelion wine and biscuits.

Tuesday, May 5. Mowed lawn and sanded it as an experiment. Terrible murder on Leeds Road. Mrs Todd of Pool Bank was assailed by a stranger who mutilated her body and cut her head off, stripping her body naked.

Saturday, May 16. To Pool to see Mr Tankard and walked back. Immense number of cyclists and motor cars passing. The dust nuisance will be awful in dry weather. Something will have to be done about it.

Thursday, May 21. Fanny and the other women in another fit of cleaning. It is the scullery today and they are in a terrible stew.

Saturday, June 6. Up to Clifton on Rate business. Coming down the road just above Carr Bank I found a trout laid on the road. It was fresh and sweet and weighed just one pound. No doubt some angler had lost it from his creel.

Sunday, June 7. Cooked trout I found last evening for breakfast. Good.

Thursday, June 25. Fanny started for Timble about 10 a.m. It was hot and I guess she would sweat and feel done up before she got there. The bridge in Otley was crowded up to dusk watching the bathers, also the new Territorial Army exercising in the Holmes with horses. Many are the attractions these summer evenings.

Friday, June 26. Very hot. All the world out of doors. Evening bathing all the thing by the bridge. The prudish object to this but that is giving way to broader views.

Tuesday, June 30. Fanny and I in town buying bedsteads and things with a view to furnishing Chapel House at Timble either to let or go to a bit ourselves.

Wednesday, July 1. Hottest day this year. Marvellous light at midnight. The northern skies were lit up with a wonderful glow and hills and trees could be seen clearly miles away. You might read small print without artificial light.

Saturday, July 4. G. Dickinson arrived at 2 and we loaded furniture which we took to Timble and Fanny and I followed on foot. Arrived about 6, then set to fixing up bedstead and preparing to take possession. Got bed ready and so a new epoch begins with a sort of half residence at Timble. We slept well but things are a bit empty and unhandy yet. The village was surprised at our unexpected arrival. Fanny staying to superintend paper-hanging.

Tuesday, July 7. Wanted to see the King on his visit to Leeds . . . but George Holmes asked me and Dorothy to ride with him to Harewood. We arrived soon after 2 p.m. George and his wife and daughter May were with us. We got a good stand around the open space in front of the park gates and stood over two hours. Carriages, motor cars and vehicles of all sorts poured in by the hundred, cyclists and pedestrians by the thousands so that Harewood never saw the like before. The procession arrived about 5 p.m. and we saw the King and Queen, but very briefly as they drove at a brisk pace. Homeward by Moortown, a very pleasant outing in fine weather. So the King's visit is over which has kept Leeds in a ferment for the past few weeks.

Friday, July 10. Miss Pankhurst in the Market Place in the evening speaking on behalf of female suffrage. She spoke very eloquently and made out a good case. Showery weather and haytime stopped for the time being.

Thursday, July 16. Came on very wet and so the poor farmers are done again. But somehow they survive these adverse strokes of fortune and come out again brisk as bottled ale.

Friday, July 24. The Territorial Army are drilling down in the bridge Holmes all along these evenings. This immense cost of war preparations seems to be a sad blot on our so-called advanced civilisation. May the time soon come when war shall be no more.

Monday, August 3. All the world is on the move for the Bank Holiday. Swimmers are sporting in the Wharfe in the hot sunshine and scores are looking on from the bridge. Vehicles of all sorts are passing to and fro and all seem bent on pleasure. I have no fancy for it so I come home to my lonely bed because all the rest are at Timble.

These August days with shortening eves
When corn is reaped and bound in sheaves
Tis then the sportsman gun in hand
Ascends the hills to high moorland
Where lonely stands the shooting house
Surrounded by the calling grouse

Saturday, August 8. Got up hot again. Much dust in the roads and motorcars are condemned by all classes, but they are still here and will stay. So what can we do? It is a very grave problem as the pleasure of walking or driving a horse on the roads is become a thing of the past.

Friday, August 14. Sale of cottage at White Horse. Old Johnny Fairburn's cottage in Fewston Bent Quarry. It made £47. Later the late George Procter's property at Timble, 123 acres put up in ten lots. Only one lot of about eight acres sold at £45 an acre to Colonel Dawson.

The weather still keeps very fine
Old Sol keeps up a steady shine
The corn is ripening in the field
And promise gives of liberal yield
The hay is housed and farmers say
They ne'er had better stacks of hay
So on the whole the season's good
Without extreme of drought or flood

Friday, September 4. My nephew, Charles Archer came about 9 with a woebegone aspect to tell us that his wife had left him. Left a note on the table yesterday saying she had gone and would not come back to Bramhope again. Left him with three little children and the poor lad to fight his way alone.

Monday, September 7. Registered death of Mrs Lee of Castley, formerly Nellie Beck. She was a healthy fresh-looking girl 30 years ago whom I in my wayward youth walked out with in a kind of sweet-hearting. She died of cancer, aged 49.

Wednesday, September 9. At home reading Dickens' *David Copperfield.* I like Dickens. His humour and pathos touches my feelings. Dickens was born the same year as my father, 1812. He died in 1870 and my father in 1875. Where are they now? Many matters of imaginary character seem to bother me just now. Things don't seem to go as I would like. I will try to look forward like Mr Micawber did for something to turn up. My chief bother is that we are outweighted with this big house of ours and I would like to get it well let and ourselves with a house more to our liking and mode of life.

Tuesday, September 15. Fanny and Dorothy arrived from Timble yesterday. I was up by 7 today, cleaned my shoes and made myself a basin of oatmeal porridge. As I write this at 8.30 a.m. Fanny and Dorothy are still in bed. They are not good at getting up in a morning but capital at keeping up late at night. We have rabbit pie to dinner.

Wednesday, September 30. Dorothy and May Holmes off by 9 to Timble blackberrying. A most beautiful still warm day. Fanny and I walked up to Carr Top to meet them. They were later than we expected but they breezed down the fields and were in famous case and full of the stirring incidents of their day out. They opened the new burial ground at Fewston today.

The days grow short but summer lingers
Full soon the chill will nip our fingers
But why repine for the evil day
From chill December will come sweet May

Thursday, October 22. Busy all day writing out Rate for Newall-with-Clifton. It causes me a great amount of work and worry but the £12 or £14 a year it brings in is very useful.

Friday, October 23. Preparing for excursion to London, that mighty centre of the Empire. What strange phases of life it presents. Some roll in wealth and pomp and pride and others grovel in poverty and degradation. Why is this inequality? Will it ever be equalised, levelled down or up?

Monday, October 26. Got all ready and cab came and took us to catch the 6.59 a.m. train to Leeds. Mr and Mrs John Kay and Mr and Mrs Lawson joined us in the trip. A young Mr Renwick, a joiner, with his wife and daughter on the train starting for Australia. Pathetic partings. Took the 8.8 train for London and arrived at 1 p.m. Cab to Kenilworth Hotel near the British Museum. Looked through the museum after dinner and then rode on an omnibus through the principal streets. Later at the Alhambra Palace Theatre. There till 11, then to hotel and bed and slept well.

Tuesday, October 27. Up at 8. Capital breakfast. Good clean house this hotel. Took train for Shepherds Bush and the Franco–British Exhibition. A marvellous place, but being a very wet day it looked as bad as it could. The Canadians seem very progressive. We looked at many of the places including the Irish Village. Left Exhibition about 6.30 and took the Tube railway to the Strand, then attended the Lyceum Theatre. The play was *Pete*. There till 11 and then to St. Pancras Station and took the 12.5 a.m. train to Leeds. It was dark and cold but we got through. The journey was not of the pleasantest. Myself, Mr Kay and Mr Lawson with our wives were all in one compartment from midnight to 6 in the morning. We took the 6.40 a.m. train from Leeds to Otley and then home well tired.

Thursday, November 12. I am 64 years old today. I am fairly active and still erect and walk with an easy swing. These birthdays seem to come round faster than they did when we were younger, but why grieve? Old Time has always been playing this game with mankind and does not seem likely to alter his ways. The great world whirls on through space and the sun and the stars answer to their appointed times. Man grovels here below in his petty ways, some rising and some falling, some coming and some going, and still we have not solved the mystery of it all.

Thursday, November 17. Fixed up delf rack in kitchen and put willow pattern dishes in. We are quite pleased and proud it looks so well.

In an ordinary sort of way
I pass most of my time away
A stretch of work, a run of play
A spell of gloom, a touch of gay
And thus the days do pass away

Tuesday, November 24. Afternoon at Clifton collecting Rates. Got £13 14*s*. Farmers grumble at the rise which has been gradually taking place this past few years. The country seems disturbed and much poverty abounds amid great wealth.

Monday, November 30. Menston in afternoon. Walked both ways. A litle frost but I tripped away quite smart. Called in to see old Joe Hannam at Menston who used to be the cattle doctor up Fewston way. He has drunk whisky and all sorts of other intoxicants all his life in great quantity, and he is now 85 years old.

Saturday, December 12. Mr Irwell, contractor, of Leeds, came with his motor car at 10 and I went with him to Middleton to look at an estate of 120 acres he has purchased. He is going to alter an old barn into a house. I came back in his car. We came back in 17 minutes. These cars are a wonderful invention, run smoothly and in a measure annihilate space. What may come in the way of flying machines will most likely to be still more wonderful.

Sunday, December 20. Home all day. Very indolent. No worship. Fanny and Dorothy attend to that.

Monday, December 21. We rendered pigs leaves today and the craps are so good.

> *When lard had been produced from the fatty leaves, the fat, in small pieces, called craps or crappins was habitually eaten cold with dry bread and salt.*

Tuesday, December 22. Interview with Mr Walker, printer, re reporting for the local paper. Varied are my pursuits from inspecting a mansion to catching a mouse.

Friday, Christmas Day. Very fine calm day almost like Spring yet a rather cutting air. Walked up Newall Carr above Clifton Lane before dinner. Fell in with congenial company. Home soon after 12 to the goose giving out a savoury smell. Dinner about 1. Goose splendid and tender.

Wednesday, December 30. Great earthquake in southern Italy. Over 100,000 reported deaths. Messina and Reggio practically destroyed. How terrible the forces of Nature do seem.

Looking back upon the year I cannot note any event of striking importance. Our lives have run along in an even tenor. The oldest member of our house, Fanny's mother, is over 74, but active and able to do useful work. She has got the Old Age Pension granted and cashed her first order for five shillings yesterday.

I come next in point of years, 64 last November. I have attended to my duties with fair punctuality and accuracy, and I trust to continue active duty for a while yet. I have had fairly good health and my income and outgo have been about the usual amounts.

Then comes Fanny, my wife. She too has been blessed with a moderate amount of good health. She has kept the house clean and in good order, cooked good meals and kept things going very well.

Last comes our only child, Dorothy, 17 last July. Grown a woman practically. She is strong and hearty and is fairly good at the piano. She would benefit if she was put into a training school as our life at home may tend to spoil her. One cannot guess ever what the lot of the young may be but I trust she may develop good common sense and fulfill her mission in life with credit.

We have no definite plans for the future but feels as if a change is coming nearer. If things go well I might retire on my superannuation allowance as Registration and Vaccination Officer, and we should let this house and go to live say at Timble or some point near to Timble. As one gets on into the sixties a sense of loneliness is felt. The companions of youth are mostly scattered by death or other causes and one has to mix with a new generation or stand apart.

1909

Friday, January 1. Last night's supper of rich things at Mr Lawson's caused indigestion and I did not feel in quite right condition this morning. Fanny and Dorothy off to Timble for a few days. Myself in town in the afternoon. Folks indulging in New Year drinks and the farmers staying after the market later than usual, some from the Timble tribe of Dickinsons. We Dickinsons are too much given to this so-called social habit and it behoves us to set our faces against excess. I have made no particular resolution for the New Year but feels as if I ought to mend my manners one way or another.

Saturday, January 2. The aftermath of the great festal season is felt in the pinch of money among those who don't save up. Few there are who practise thrift in comparison with those of years ago . . . And yet

> Dull the days and so is trade
> Where is now the roving blade
> That used to romp at feast and fair?
> He's passed away I do declare

Wednesday, January 20. Party at our house. We have got into the connections and are obliged to keep it up. If we take invitations we must give them back so the thing goes on . . . We drew up a programme and each person sang, recited or did something. We had a good old Yorkshire ham boiled and home-cured tongue and other etceteras and we had a right jolly time up to 1.30 a.m.

Monday, February 8. Wrote letter to Mr Speight, the historian, re Thomas Hardcastle, the founder of the cotton trade at Bolton in Lancashire. I trust I gave him the right man, born at West End about 1767.

> Rain and sleet with boisterous wind
> A trying time for humankind
> The days are short the nights are dark
> And silent yet the soaring lark

Tuesday, February 23. Cold peevish weather. Town a bit in forenoon. My various duties keep me on watch yet I have much leisure time which I do not utilise as I ought to do.

Eight hours of rest I take in bed
Or nine sometimes if truth be said
My appetite is very fair
My mind is not too full of care

Sunday, February 28. Lantern lecture at Congregational School on Jerusalem, by Mr Arthur Duncan. Not very good as the views were not well shown.

Monday, March 1. Up at 7.30. Kindled fire and cooked bacon. Aunt Mary and Dorothy then came down. Strong argument with Aunt Mary re earthquakes. We had rather high words and almost a serious difference. Fanny came back about noon, very poorly.

Soon the Spring will come again
And flowers will bloom in field and lane
The birds will sing in ghyll and dell
And lambs will play on moorland fell

Thursday, March 4. Very nasty weather with biting cutting raw frosty sort of air. Conditions generally are very bad for the poor. Many are out of work and hard put to get the necessities of life.

Saturday, March 6. It is 23 years today since my dear mother died after a life of hard work from which I profited, chiefly in my moods of industry and thrift.

Monday, March 8. Vast quantity of snow lying on the ground. Piled up on all sides in Otley like windrows of hay. Evening at concert at Mechanics Institute.

O for a touch of the Spring sunshine
And the balm of a soft west wind
To wander where grows the sweet woodbine
In an Eden where Adam sinned

Wednesday, March 17. The country is startled today by finding that Germany is fast rising in naval strength and is already almost equal to England. This must not be and the national spirit is roused and is likely to assert itself.

Saturday, March 27. After dinner started for Timble. A motorcar passing containing a party of three gentlemen all three sheets in the wind invited me to ride so I was up at Four Lane Ends in no time. Evening at Parish Meeting in the Library. Supper at Sun Inn, Norwood and all night at sister Mary Ann's.

Monday, April 12. Fanny, Dorothy and Aunt Mary at Timble. Slept badly, having milk to supper the cause of it, I think. It is a change to be alone and one feels it after having three aggressive self-opinionated women in the house all asserting their rights.

Tuesday, April 13. Alone all last night but slept better. Went over to the Refreshment House and had a sixpenny plate of beef. Fanny and Dorothy arrived from Timble about dusk. They had walked all the way in the wet.

Saturday, April 24. Walter Roundell took Fanny and me to Timble in his trap. Meeting of the Library trustees at 3 p.m., parish meeting in the Library at night. They raised my salary as assistant overseer from £6 a year to £7. Laura Lister of the Inn was elated at the return of her sweetheart Mr Chamberlain tonight after an absence of several months.

Thursday, April 29. Up at 8. We like bed, all of us, but don't hurry to it at night. Writing at Rate work. Our women are nearly done cleaning down which is a blessing.

> This cleaning down comes sure as Spring
> It is a most annoying thing
> When Nature dons her gayest dress
> Our home's a contrast — what a mess!
> No peace I have by day or night
> I cannot do a thing that's right

Thursday, May 20. Afternoon in town. Chief local topic was the paternity case against William Ramsden of Folly Hall, who was charged by a West End young woman who had been a servant at Philips of Snowden with being the father of her child. She had no corroborative evidence and the case was dismissed.

Monday, May 24. Hardly any sleep last night. Sick and vomiting. Fanny and Dorothy still at Timble. Two parties here for registration business. Made five shillings in certificates. Gave a poor tramp tea and some bread and bacon. He was going to lodge at the Workhouse casual ward where severe task work is to do on bread and water and to stay two nights. I pitied the man and it almost seemed more than he could hope for to be liberated.

Friday, May 28. Fanny and Dorothy home from Timble. Market routine but in addition a Liberal van with a fiery orator in support of Free Trade and other Liberal principles. A large crowd and frequent opposition but all passed off good-humouredly.

Monday, June 7. All the world seems to be going mad on dreadnoughts and militarism. The Territorials are training down by Otley Bridge almost every evening, and a fighting spirit seems to be in the air. Folks seem to feel something startling is going to happen.

Thursday, June 10. Rent audit today and there was plenty of whisky to be had. G. Currer made me a strong glass which upset me and I had to retire in disorder. Glad to get home and to bed. I understand that Currer used gin instead of water in my whisky, hence the mischief.

Wednesday, June 23. Grass growing very fast now the rain having come. The farmers are contented and silent for a bit now. But they will soon be complaining again, you bet.

> The farmer would grouse if it rained grass and corn
> To natter and grumble he seems to be born

Monday, June 28. Took 4.15 train to Manningham with Dorothy who is under-going special treatment at the Electro Institution for a lameness in her hip or leg. After the treatment we ran down by tram into Bradford and had tea at Lyons Cafe.

Monday, July 5. Took 1.39 train, Dorothy to Otley and I to Esholt after Dorothy's treatment in Manningham. I went to meet the Bradford Sewage Engineer re alteration to the Commercial Inn at Esholt. Walked up to Guiseley which is on tiptoe about the electric trams being newly opened to Guiseley and there is a 20-minute service right through to Leeds.

Tuesday, July 13. Hay harvest drags on slowly. Part farmers drunk from over Timble way. Met Mr Stott and John Kay re idea of buying a field at Carr Bank Bottom. I am to make an offer to Mr Fawkes.

My wife says I'm too old to speculate
But I say now's the time or I'll be late
The adage says its better late than never
Its best I say to be progressing ever.

Friday, July 16. Usual market day incidental. Farmers lively. A man selling stack covers and other farm things in front of White Horse drew a crowd. Close by was a Punch and Judy show. Lecture on the Cross on teetotalism.

Aviation is all the talk just now
They venture on the wing if favoured winds do blow
On Sunday last a Frenchman flew across the Straits
And landed safe at Dover, well favoured by the Fates
Poor Latham who tried and failed so late
May now sit down and curse his adverse fate.

Louis Bleriot (1872–1936) flew the English Channel from Calais to Dover in 37 minutes on 25 July, 1909. Latham is now forgotten except in records of pioneering days of flying.

Wednesday, July 28. Up at Clifton on Rate business. Money is scarce and everybody complains of the high Rates which makes my job very unpleasant. The Australian cricketers are beating England at Manchester and Latham has again failed to fly the Channel, so poor old England seems about done for. But I don't think the old lion is worn out yet.

Tuesday, August 3. Helping nephew G. Archer with his hay and we put over an acre into good lap-cock which held us tight up to 8 p.m. My nephew is not quite so pushful as I used to be when I had the place, but he possesses some good points. Looked in to see Uncle George Dickinson who is 85 and his wife Bess also 85. They have been married about 63 years. I remember them as the busiest and strongest couple in the village, but now alas they are old and feeble.

Monday, August 9. Summer has come indeed. At home making out vaccination returns. Everybody else busy with haytime.

O, what a whiff and whaff is life
Whether or not you've got a wife
Ralph Wilson, single, by himself
Is anxious adding to his wealth
George Holmes with family and wife
Finds not what he had hoped from life
Myself who lives the medium way
Have laboured on till old and gray
To see how vain is life's young dream
Which rushes like a mountain stream
On to the ocean's mystic shore
Lost in the depths to be no more
To be no more — that's not the truth
Both man and streams renew their youth.

Friday, August 13. Still very fine and dry. Pulled first lot of green peas and had some for dinner. Sent some to Timble for Sunday.

All the world is walking out
Or swimming lively as a trout
Lovers wander in the lanes
Cripples reck not aches and pains
Old and young and low and high
Love the open air and sky

Wednesday, August 18. Thirty-four years ago this evening my father went out with his gun to shoot wood pigeons. He was always a keen sportsman. He did not return home and as the evening wore on mother and I got anxious and later friends joined us and we went down the fields and down to Swinsty. At last we found him, laid on the Braid Lane where he had dropped down dead. No doubt from heart failure.

What changes occur as the years roll by
In old days folk walked but in these days they fly
But with all man's inventions, death still claims his due
Who can say which is best, the old or the new?
Men were healthy and strong in the days that are past
Now man's physique is weakened by going too fast.

Friday, August 27. Market as usual. The Budget League were in the town. I heard speeches on the gramophone by Mr Asquith,

Winston Churchill and Lloyd George. Also two or three good live speakers all in favour of the Budget.

Friday, September 3. Meeting of trustees of Timble Library. The funds get lower and by and by I suppose we shall run short and then something will have to be done. Walked up to Clifton in the evening to post notices.

The air is sweet up on the hills
The waters clear down in the ghylls
And life is simple, calm and sweet
Free from the slum and dirty street.

Met cousin Thomas Dickinson and bade adieu to him. He sails for the United States on Tuesday next. Poor Tom.

The Pole by Cook and now by Peary
Has been discovered to be dreary
There must be something queer about it
And many seem to rather doubt it.

Robert E. Peary (1856–1920) American explorer discovered the North Pole on April 6, 1909. He was challenged by a prior claim from fellow American explorer Frederick Albert Cook (1865–1940), who said he reached the Pole in 1908. Peary's claim to have discovered the Pole was recognised and later verified scientifically.

Thursday, September 16. Sale at Whellam's drapery shop just below the Black Bull Inn. Shops are doing badly just now. Cleaned three pairs of shoes and made myself a basin of oatmeal porridge.

Saturday, September 25. After accounts and overseers work at the Liberal Club an hour perusing the newspapers. I read a lot in the paper to the detriment of my eyesight which is getting very weak. I shall have to wear spectacles for walking outside. I can hardly distinguish people across the street, and reading with my ordinary spectacles makes them ache.

Wednesday, September 29. Trade bad all round here in Otley. Property is down, but the necessaries of life rather up. The Budget is fighting its way through the House of Commons but the Lords are expected to throw it out.

Monday, October 4. Not so well. Stomach again out of order due partly to eating too heartily of roast veal yesterday.

The weather seems to get no better
The times are wet and getting wetter
Up Timble way some hay's still out
One asks what they have been about
Surely the hay might have been got
And not till now been left to rot

Thursday, October 5. Another wild wet day. Aunt Mary cannot sleep through extreme aching in her left arm and shoulder.

The trout will spawn in Timble Ghyll
When days are moist and mild and still
Long years ago I often went
Down to the ghyll with good intent
To catch the trout in still clear pools
Though I knew it was against the rules

Monday, October 11. Looked in at ILP Room in Station Road where Captain Boyd Carpenter, son of the Bishop of Ripon, was addressing the Labour Party on the folly of Socialism. I was only in about ten minutes as it was crowded and very stuffy. The speaker seemed to be in earnest and had something to say.

The Budget now is all the talk
Wherever men do ride or walk
Some says its based on evolution
While others say its revolution.
I say its clauses first will give
The working class a chance to live
And share the wealth due to their toil
In delving stone or getting 'coil'
The dukes have got the cream till now
Will they give in or face a row?

Tuesday, October 19. Aviation Week is going on at Doncaster and at Blackpool and being the first exhibition of flying in England much stir is occasioned thereby.

Friday, October 22. Attended meeting of Plans Committee.

Dinner at Pawson's eating house. Small plate of beef and potatoes, sixpence. Cup of coffee and bun twopence. Eightpence the lot and plenty.

Friday, November 12. I feel impressed with the stern fact that I am 65 years old today. Surely this means I am entering the mansion where a cosy corner chair and rest invite relaxation. I almost feel inclined to seek relief from some of my work. I might claim superannuation on my vaccination office and registration appointments which might bring me about £24 per year. At present, however, I must hold on.

Thursday, November 18. Not up till 8.10. We like our bed so warm and soft but we rise keen for breakfast and business. Then I read the paper, attend to correspondence, and today busy with planning matters. At Liberal Club a while reading more papers. The Lords have thrown out the Budget and an election will come within the New Year. I rather think that tariff reform will prevail now or after as we are alone among the nations in our free trade policy.

Friday, November 19. Otley Statutes and a fine dry day with frosty air and sunshine. Little hiring is now done in the street as it used to be. The main attraction now seems to be the street quacks bawling out their story, drinking in the public houses and visiting the Fair in the Licks which was crowded at night with young folks. To me now it looks like vanity and foolishness, but I don't forget that I once was young and foolish as any of them.

Monday, December 13. George Dickinson of Sowerby Farm, Timble, called about 6.30 and left 23 sovereigns for half a years rent for Sowerby Farm. I am reading *A Thousand Miles on the Nile.* Fascinating. Keeps me keen of interest and wonder how these ancient peoples did such wondrous work.

Saturday, Christmas Day. Our women busy cooking goose. Two bands of music playing around. Several boys and girls saluted for coppers. Day fine with snow around.

Thursday, December 30. Roast pig chine to dinner. Very tasty. Up to Clifton to register a birth for Robert Newbould. Poor Robert. He has been twice to Australia, the wife of his youth being with him on his voyages as has been in England faithfully up to some 18 months ago when she died at the age of 75 never having had issue. Robert is about 70. His late wife's niece came to keep house for him, a stout young woman who is parted from her husband. Result, a baby boy to Robert. Poor old Bob, so foolish in his old age. Still it is procreation which he had not done before for lack of the proper utensils. And folks talk.

Friday, December 31. At Mr Lawson's, tailor of Kirkgate, Fanny and I his guests for supper. Within a stone's throw of the Parish Church and we heard the stroke of the church clock bell strike out the old care-laden year directly followed by a merry peal ringing in the new with all it may mean.

The past year has been very ordinary to me and us . . . My round of duties as Registrar of Births and Deaths and Vaccination Officer, Plans and Building Inspector, Assistant Overseer and Rate Collector for Timble Great and Newall-with-Clifton, together with other small duties keep me pretty well going especially when the garden work is added . . .

I feel it is not wise to live in this large house which means more work and expense than is needful for us. Our outlay is part over £3 per week, but we only have the one child and we are not anxious to save money at the cost of a fair measure of comfort . . .

The New Year is now before us and if God spares us to see it through I trust that I may be enabled to carry out the work which falls in my way . . . I cannot hope to set the rivers on fire or paint the town red as I might have done if I had followed the bent of my ambition when I was young.

O may we walk in wisdoms ways
And make the best of future days
So that when this life's course is run
It may be said of us 'Well done.'

1910

Saturday, January 1. A few faint New Year resolves made to break. Still it feels sort of hopeful to make them. It shows there is just a spark of the right thing left.

Thursday, January 6. Walked to Menston to inspect houses, then train down and called at Duncan's committee rooms re the election matters. The election is all the talk now it is fraught with grave issues and savage instincts will be roused. I shall vote Liberal as before but am just a bit favourable to tariff reform.

Friday, January 7. Whitaker Thompson the Conservative candidate addressed the market folk from the White Horse balcony at 1.45 p.m. He talks fluently enough but the principles are the old sort.

Saturday, January 8. Fanny and Dorothy busy cleaning. They do belabour this thing, but it is better than dirt.

Monday, January 10. General Election all the talk. Duncan the Liberal and Thompson the Conservative are running for this Division. I think Duncan is safe but the leading questions are out of the ordinary run so we cannot feel sure.

How it will go is quite hard to say
Each one is sure his is the right way
Tariff Reform the Conservative plank
Free Trade pervading the Liberal rank
With 'Down with the Lords' and 'Cut their veto'
There's a terrible hubbub wherever you go

Monday, January 17. About 10 p.m. went over to Liberal Club and joined in the excitement as the polls' results came in. The Liberals were jubilant though losing seats. They feel they can spare them and still go back to office.

Wednesday, January 19. About 11 a.m. went to North Parade School and voted for James H. Duncan, the Liberal candidate.

About 10 p.m. when Fanny and I went into town the streets were crowded about the clubs and Mechanics Insititute. It was about midnight when the poll was declared. Duncan was elected by a majority of 1,901, the actual figures being J. Duncan 6,911 and W. Whitaker Thompson, 5,010. Tremendous excitement at the Liberal Club. A fine moonlight night. Got home near 2 a.m.

The Liberal landslide in the 1906 election had given Sir H. Campbell-Bannerman a majority of 356. In the election in January 1910 with H.H. Asquith leading the party the Liberal majority was reduced to 124.

Monday, January 24. Good breakfast of pig cheek and coffee. Snowing and very cold. In house all day. We elders stick to the fire.

Tuesday, January 25. Saw the new comet this evening. Not Halley's, but a brand new one. It is only visible in the evening for a short time on the western horizon. Its tail is pointing up.

Friday, January 28. Very heavy fall of snow. Nobody stirring only the milkman. Otley market attendance the thinnest on record. Only two or three on horseback came from Timble way. Only two or three butchers stalls out. Other stallholders didn't turn up. The town wore a woebegone aspect and folk were off home in good time.

Tuesday, February 8. In bed all day. Dr Williamson came and says I am suffering from catarrh of the stomach. Much pain at pit of stomach and can eat nothing, only milk. Useful lesson in care of what I eat and drink.

Friday, February 11. Milk and sops to breakfast. A little better in appetite. Fish to dinner.

The day was dull and pains severe
Depressed my hopes and made me fear
That life's thin thread was giving way
So dark and hopeless was the day.

Monday, February 14. Up at 8.30. Much better and appetite returning. Porridge to breakfast, mutton steak to dinner, poached egg on toast to tea. So am going on very well.

Tuesday, March 1. Trade dull and great rumours about

emigration. Many going from Otley to Canada, but not all who talk of emigrating do it. The young man's fancy often roams that way but he stays at home.

Wednesday, March 9. With Fanny and Dorothy on 11.15 train to Bradford. Then tram to Allerton and on to Thomas Procter's at Chellow Heights. And it is on the heights on a cold windy day like this. Tom has ten children all at home, some grown up and the rest in rotation. Back to the tram in a blinding blizzard and the 8.35 train home. Dorothy consulted an eye specialist and we paid a guinea for a pair of spectacles.

Good Friday, March 25. A most beautiful day, dry and sunshiny. Many people passing about on holiday bent. Working myself in garden on little jobs.

The Springtime comes round
With sunshine and sound
Of birds gaily singing
And flowers upspringing
All Nature rejoices
In various voices

Tuesday, March 29. Sowed all garden seeds. Very tiring work. Feel almost done up. Fanny and Dorothy commenced cleaning down so I must keep as quiet as possible.

Monday, April 11. In town to buy a bedstead. We bought one at Jackson's Stores, a rather showy thing for £2 17*s* 6*d*. They brought it and set it up in the evening and we pulled the old wooden one down.

Tuesday, April 12. Up at 7.30 after the first night in our fine flash burnished glittering new bedstead. Our women changing feather bed into new tic. Self writing in forenoon and then to Clifton re overseers business. 'Wait and see' is just now a catch phrase introduced by Mr Asquith the Premier. I get oatmeal porridge twice a day and my stomach is not so frequently disordered as a while ago, but we must wait and see.

The Spring is coming all agree
But yet we have to wait and see
The cuckoo's song heard from the tree
But yet we have to wait and see
At last we all shall have to dee
Long may we have to wait and see

Thursday, April 14. To town for fish for dinner. Two pounds of aik, price fourpence per pound.

Friday, April 15. Fanny, Dorothy and Lotty Pennington to Ilkley by 1.49 train to attend a musical competition. Dorothy had to play a pianoforte solo. She did pretty well I suppose but got no prize, as young ladies from the high schools were competing who had superior advantage.

Monday, April 18. Depressed through indigestion and no heart for anything. Cannot recuperate as I used to do, but I must not get downhearted. Maybe life has a little plum or two for me yet.

Saturday, April 23. Great ado about football. Otley in the final for the Yorkshire Cup plays Hull at Harrogate. Otley won and the town was seething in excitement all the evening. To me it looks like foolery, but I am old.

Wednesday, May 4. Good breakfast of bacon and egg. Roundell's boy with trap at 9.30. Drove to Lawnswood Cemetery and inspected work there. Then to the Manor House at Adel, and on to Moss Hall at Alwoodley about drainage. Then to Arthington and Pool. It was also my day for registration at Pool so I sent the trap home and I staied till 6 p.m., having to meet Mr Lax at 5.30 re drainage. Walked home from Pool. Yesterday I walked to Menston both ways. My feet get tired with a few miles. My heels get to ache from what cause I don't know but it comes on painful. It may be the years of my pilgrimages. Anyhow the fact is so.

Friday, May 6. A wild and stormy day for Otley Show with snow and hail and thunder. No comfort in the field at any point. About the poorest Show day I ever remember. It was starved out.

Saturday, May 7. Death of the King in all the papers this morning having taken place at about 11.45 last night. Thus ends a life conspicuously to the fore all my time. Only about three years older than me . . . Genuine sorrow is felt on all hands at the end of a good ruler of our vast Empire. But the King still lives and we will hope he will turn out as good as his father, Edward the Peacemaker.

Tuesday, May 10. Proclamation of the new monarch, George V at Mechanics Institute about 1.30. Read out by Mr Brogan, a working stone mason, who is chairman of Otley Urban Council and he did it very well. A vast concourse assembled to hear it.

Monday, May 23. Many people on Weston Lane looking for

Halley's Comet. It was not very distinct but I could see it very well with my field glasses. It seemed to be a fuzzy sort of light without head or tail.

Thursday, June 2. Late in the evening I took a stray cat which had tried to come home with me up Farnley Woods way and left it there. I felt like commiting murder as I stole out on my cruel errand.

Sunday, June 5. Many people on the move after church services. This is the popular parade and fashion shows itself in gay and showy colours.

Tuesday, June 14. Fanny's and Dorothy's washing day so I went over to town for some mutton and new potatoes. Half a shoulder of mutton at 8½*d* per pound, new potatoes 1½*d.* per pound, loaf of bread threepence. Then home. I am just kept in nice easy work with my various official appointments, but I would like a place where we could keep a few hens.

Thursday, June 16. To town in forenoon and left £20 in the bank. It is very nice to have a good balance at the bank for emergencies. Clipped privet hedge but spent rather an idle day. Some days I am that way and then may take a fit of industry. I was always a bit that way partly I think because I was not put to regular work in my youthful days.

Long twilight extends into the night
The moon goes up and makes more light
Down in the Licks the cinematograph show
With bells and steam music kicks up a row
Here in our garden all is peace and calm
Neither too cool nor is it too warm.

Sunday, June 26. Walked up to Mr Thackwray's at Timble Ings with Nathan who has built a big new barn and done all the work himself. Crossed the fields to Summerhills. A pheasant fluttered off her nest. Eleven eggs in and Nathan took them to hatch out under a hen.

Friday, July 1. Attended sale of farm at White Horse belonging to the late Mrs Irish of Hardisty Hill Top, Fewston. Made £620, a poor price considering what land formerly sold for. All the talk just now is about the Johnson and Jeffries fight in the United States.

Negro Jack Johnson (1878–1946), won the heavyweight boxing championship of the world by knocking out James J. Jeffries (1875–1953). Lost title to Jess Willard in 1915.

Tuesday, July 12. Very fine weather and hay-making going on wonderfully well. In the evening Mr Nicholson, cashier in the London City and Midland Bank at Otley took me on the river in his boat. Very pleasant sail up to Duncans Mill. Three glasses of ale with him later at the Horse Shoes. Swimming in the river in full go.

Thursday, July 14. Washerwoman here as our women are not very well. I am in better than usual health and appetite and am starting to grow side whiskers, but Fanny says they will be white and make me look old. I can shave them off if I want to but I think they will strengthen my eyesight.

Tuesday, July 19. Fanny and I took the 11.15 train to Guiseley, then on to Kirkstall Abbey for the first time. Impressed with the magnitude and splendour of this fine old ruin and felt thankful for the sermons in stones which we inherit from the Romish church. Yet we seem to hate the Catholic folks. We owe most of our finest architecture and art works to the religious spirit. Tram on to Leeds and good dinner at the County Cafe. Then tram and motorbus to Adel. Inspected house and then back to Leeds. Tea there, then Empire Music Hall from 7 to 9. Supper at cafe and 10.10 train home. Saw much stirring life. Leeds is becoming more and more important as a metropolitan centre.

Monday, July 25. Rabbit pie and tea to breakfast. Mrs Eastwood came by 9 to pay rent of £6 17*s* 6*d* for the quarter.

Monday, August 1. Ideal Bank Holiday weather. Crippen has been arrested.

Dr Crippen was sailing to the United States with his mistress Ethel Le Neve when a radio message enabled police to arrest him on landing and charge him with the murder of his wife in London.

Tuesday, August 2. Stomach out of order again. It recurs do as I may, although I rather think I abuse it when I feel well. I must have a strong bump of alimentiveness, if that is the right word.

> *It is. Alimentiveness: That which impels an animal to seek food.*

Friday, September 16. Town in the afternoon. Chief attraction was a voluble man selling sponges. He sold many hundreds at half a dozen for a shilling.

Thursday, September 29. Porridge to breakfast. I am eating a good deal of porridge all along and so far I feel better in health and appetite than I did a few months ago. Went for walk after porridge supper. Much life astir, pianos playing on the terraces, lovers walking out, topers drinking, a few steady goers like myself taking a quiet stroll. The stars shone brightly. I look on them with wonder and stand amazed at the mystery of Creation.

Sunday, October 2. Aunt Mary and Dorothy to chapel. Roast leg of lamb to dinner. Came on wet so I kept in reading.

> It hits the farmer right and left
> Destroying both his warp and weft
> If this years crop should fail like last
> The Rubicon of hope is passed
> And farmers hopes though never high
> Would with the aviators fly

Wednesday, October 12. Sale at Leathley, Mr Weatherill's. Bought five books for one shilling. Carlyle's *French Revolution.* Very cheap. Porridge to supper. I like porridge nowadays.

Wednesday, October 19. Up at Workhouse for census particulars. Jones the Workhouse Master and his wife the Matron and their boy are all very fat and jolly. The inmates are mostly thin and melancholy. The trial of Dr Crippen has begun and the newspapers are full of it. Wellman and his crew have essayed to cross the Atlantic in a dirigible balloon but have failed.

Wednesday, November 2. Cold touched our bed during the night. Winter is looking over the hills. Took 1.6 train to Pool and registered one birth, illegitimate. A pretty girl of 19. Fanny and Dorothy went to Bramhope.

My wife's away just for the day
So for a time I get my way
A change is pleasant now and then
Though then I have to cook missen

Thursday, November 3. At Mechanics Institute in evening for lecture by Dr Fison on wireless telegraphy. Very ably and vividly delivered.

Monday, November 7. Letter to say that my cousin Thomas Dickinson died this morning at a quarter to five. Thus is broken another link in my youthful associations though Tom was never a very boon companion. About a year ago he along with some of his family went to America, but that was disastrous and all came back and settled in Bradford.

Saturday, November 12. My birthday, I am 66. Now I must be getting old and I feel it. Very bad all day with catarrh of the stomach. Well, we cannot evade the toll of time.

Saturday, November 19. Serious illness begins, by far the most serious of my life. About midnight after catarrhal sickness commenced to vomit blood with a large quantity of other black nasty matter. Dr Williamson came early in the morning. To bed and cold water with white of egg to begin with. Fears of a growth on stomach.

Saturday, November 26. Up by 11 and sat by fire in bedroom till 10 p.m. Very comfortable. Fanny doing registration work as my deputy. Doctor comes alternate days.

Monday, December 5. Much better. Down in house and fair hearty. On milk plasma.

Tuesday, December 6. Fair night's rest. Up at 9.30. Gaining strength. Sago gruel to breakfast, rice pudding to dinner.

Wednesday, December 7. Cup of cocoa and egg with dry toast to breakfast. Beef tea to dinner. Milk and teacake to tea. Milk for supper. Brother Charles brought two young pigeons for me but the doctor forebade me eating them.

Wednesday, December 14. General Election contest in Otley Division between Duncan and Thompson. I walked over and voted for Duncan, the Liberal M.P. and candidate. Fanny and Dorothy over in town to hear result but before they returned we knew that

Duncan had won as the mill whistle was set going in a victorious manner.

> *In May, 1910 Asquith's Liberal Government had introduced the Parliament Bill to deprive the House of Lords of all power over money Bills and restricting it to a suspensive veto on other legislation of two successive sessions. It followed Opposition tactics of using the Conservative majority in the House of Lords to prevent reforms passed by the elected Liberal majority in the Commons, a device that reached a climax with the rejection of Lloyd George's 'Peoples Budget' of 1909. The Lords sought to amend the Parliament Bill out of all recognition. Parliament was again dissolved and the second General Election in December 1910 confirmed the Liberals in power with a majority increased from 124 to 126. The Bill was passed by the Lords in August 1911 after King George V had guaranteed that he would, if necessary, create 250 Liberal peers to ensure its passage.*

Thursday, December 22. Christmas preparations to the fore, but a gloom is cast over the scene by a terrible colliery accident near Bolton. 350 lives lost.

Friday, December 23. Busy registering in forenoon. Made 7*s* in certificate fees.

Saturday, December 24. Women very busy cleaning up and getting all spic and span for Christmas. Went into town in forenoon and invested in apples and oranges. I am pretty hearty but I don't indulge in much meat. Milky diet suits me best.

Sunday, Christmas Day. Fine open weather. A few boys and girls round for coppers. Walked up Carr before dinner. Only ordinary dinner. Goose reserved for tomorrow. Quite a lot of Christmas cards. This habit grows.

Saturday, December 31. Very nice day. Town in forenoon, at bank and Union offices Liberal Club and at George Holmes'. Fanny off to Timble and Aunt Mary and Dorothy and I sat up till midnight and saw the New Year in.

Time rolls on and the years seem to pass over more swiftly. I thank God I have been permitted to see the end of the year with recovered health. My income and expenditure have been much as usual, but we could easily save a lot more if we were in a smaller house . . . Sensational developments in various ways may be looked for in the coming year. Flying machines will figure largely no doubt. Electrical appliances will make a show and inventive faculties will be more than usually active I predict. Amid it all may we keep calm and do the best we can.

1911

Enter a New Year. Fine open Spring-like weather. Trade in staple industries in Otley is pretty good. The building trade nil and all outdoor work is very slack. Many houses are empty. Property is very low in value and sales are very difficult. Money is sensitive and fears this Socialism which is very apparent. All will come round again I think with the swing of the pendulum.

Sunday, January 1. Up at 8, washed and dressed and then walked up Carr. Fanny at Timble.

Thursday, January 5. Walked to Menston and inspected work there. Then walked home. I think this walking does me good. Very good appetite all along now. I take no alcohol and hardly any meat but of lighter foods I can eat very heartily. I drink only cocoa. Building trade very bad. Masons cannot get work.

Friday, January 13. I have been hauled over the coals by the Plans Committee and by misrepresentation and lying I was made to look guilty of actions of which I was entirely innocent. These blows come upon us in the course of our lives. Dark days overshadow us and we feel for a time unable to help ourselves.

> Ups and downs are here our lot
> Until we fill the final plot

Tuesday, January 24. Breakfast of cocoa, butter and bread, then in town on errand or two at shoemakers, tailors and architects. Dinner of cold beef and potatoes with cream after and sweet cake. Town again before 5 o'clock and then pot of cocoa, butter and bread and toasted cheese. Fanny and Dorothy washing.

Monday, February 20. Fanny and I at Wesleyan Chapel when the coffin arrived for William Beecroft's funeral. Then to the cemetery. A large attendance and all respectable and in order. I have known William all through our lives. He lived at Grove House, Fewston, but used to be at Ridge Top, Timble. I fought with him as a boy, and courted his sister Emma who was a sweet girl but foolish.

Tuesday, February 21. Wild and wet in the evening, but I had good fire, good lights and good literature and oatmeal porridge with oatmeal from Eli Dale, his own oatmeal made at Crags Mill, Norwood.

Tuesday, March 21. Very cold east wind. Took 1.6 train to Pool to inspect foundations of a building, and walked home. Terribly shy wind. I stood it very well though. Think I am gaining strength again.

These days so dark will soon go by
And we shall hail a sunny sky
When everything will jump for joys
And even old men feel like boys

Monday, April 3. Ham and egg to breakfast. Hearty and a fine morning. All alert and active. Dorothy and I started 8.20 to collect census schedules for the Newall part of Otley this side of the Wharfe. Over 80 dwellings. We were at it up to 4 p.m. Fanny started at the same time to collect for the old part of Newall-with-Clifton. All pretty well tired at the finish.

Thursday, April 20. Packed up census papers ready for dispatch by train. Others ready for delivery to Mr Newstead the superintendent registrar. It has been a tedious business.

Tuesday, May 2. Sowed peas and other small seeds. Our women coming near a close with cleaning down. Thanks be for that

No peace at home when cleaning down
So off I pop into the town

Tuesday, May 9. Glorious sunshine and warmth. Our folks storming the last entrenchment of dust and cobwebs. It is the scullery and I think it cannot hold out longer than tomorrow. Hurrah, hurrah, hurrah.

Saturday, May 13. Changed the position of our barometer to make room for an umbrella stand which I bought at brother Charles' sale.

Saturday, May 20. At Union offices and drew money for census work, £22 15*s* 4*d*. Shall now have to pay the enumerators . . . Drove to Norwood. Called at Jos. Gills and paid for census enumeration, then to Fewston and paid Fred Pennington. On to Hopper Lane and paid C. Powell for census work. Went on to Timble re Rate business.

> The summer days have come once more
> And trade begins once more to soar
> The crops abundant progress make
> And working folks don't want for cake.

Friday, May 26. At 6.30 at sale of Ridge Top Farm, Timble. Ben Rollinson, a former Timble resident and native bought it for £925.

Sunday, May 28. Tremendously hot sun shone but I staied in house all day. Read Shakespeare's tragedy of *Hamlet.* How this Shakespeare has sounded the heights and depths of all things.

Wednesday, May 31. Upset with heat and may be affected by casting my pants and flannel belt but it was too hot to wear them. A brisk thunder shower came in afternoon and Nature fairly jumped with joy to drink it in.

Thursday, June 1. Roundell's son came with trap and we drove for Adel. Inspected house there then drove to Moortown and inspected house there. Drove home by way of Harewood Park and got permission at the lodge and drove right through the park which is near 2,000 acres with woods and lake and mansion. A lordly domain too much for one man to own.

Thursday, June 22. Coronation Day. Dull morning with drizzly showers but it cleared up into a fine and sunny afternoon. People assembled in the Market Place and marched headed by a Band of Music to the big flat field by the bridge. They came in thousands till the field was one mass of humanity. Punch and Judy, conjuring, greasy pole competition, juvenile races, and a grand performance of Old England at a specially erected stage. At 10 p.m. a monster fire on the Chevin. Houses and shops decorated and illuminated in pretty designs.

Friday, June 23. Another day of festivity. Old folks tea at Mechanics Institute. Fanny there in official capacity as a steward. Two thousand children at free treat to cinematograph entertainment.

Sunday, July 9. Spent night at Sowerby Farm. Up at 8 and capital breakfast of ham and two eggs. A young man from Leeds and I walked to Timble Ings. The air was bracing and there were mushrooms, rabbits and grouse in the picturesque moorland. Very enjoyable.

Tuesday, July 11. Too hot to stir out. Haymakers need only cut the grass and it is hay in 24 hours. Not a cloud in the sky and the sun blazing like fire. Well, let us be thankful who can take it in the shade.

Friday, July 21. Still oppressively hot and no sign of rain. The pastures are turning.

Monday, July 24. All the talk now about the flying contest for a £10,000 prize. Thousands at Harrogate and ten thousand motorcars estimated to be there. Fanny and Dorothy and Aunt Mary there but they failed to see the flyers.

Thursday, August 3. The heat radiates from the stones so there is no getting out of it. The land is parched, the pastures brown and bare and everything suffering from lack of moisture. I cannot stand it when the sun blazes in full meridian force so I keep indoors through the heat of the day and turns out in the evening.

Wednesday, August 9. Hotter than ever. The sun blazes mercilessly so that the earth is like a frying pan or some hissing matter. Fanny and Dorothy at gramophone concert on the Wharfe. These concerts are given by Mr Nicholson, a young bank cashier from a boat on the river whilst the audience fringes the river in the Little Park and on the bridge.

Wednesday, August 16. Strike rumours now all the talk. It seems to be a national rising. Much of the railway service is dislocated and in many cases at a standstill. The outlook is ominous. Seething discontent is in the air. Meanwhile the King is having glorious sport shooting on the moors at Bolton Abbey.

Saturday, August 19. Great railway strike all the talk. Hardly any train service to and from Otley. The public will not stand it quietly much longer.

Monday, August 21. Rain fell heavily during the night, a Godsend all round.

Wednesday, August 23. Fanny and Dorothy by wagonette to Timble by 8, going with Sunday School trip to Harrogate. Fanny tries so hard to keep the little Sunday School at Timble going.

The railway strike is all the talk
It seems we soon may have to walk
Much as our grandpas used to do
Before there was a railway co.

Monday, September 11. The staple trades of Otley seem to be prosperous all along now but the small shopkeepers appear to be doing badly and several shops are unoccupied. The building trade is bad and casual labour is difficult to get. Property is at a serious discount and selling is out of the question except at ruinous loss. Thus stand affairs this September month. A dispute between France and Germany about Morocco keeps the nations anxious and talk of war is rife. Strikes are in the air on all hands and a general feeling of unrest prevails. We are in the hands of the Universal Ruler and will trust to His good providence.

On 1 July, 1911 the German gunboat Panther was sent to Agadir, a small port on the Atlantic coast of Morocco, allegedly to protect German interests menaced by French expansion in Morocco. The German Foreign Minister thought a show of strength would gain compensation for Germany. This exercise in German naval power, so close to Gibraltar and Britain's vital trade routes alarmed London, and on 21 July Lloyd George, then Chancellor of the Exchequer, uttered a strong warning to Germany in a speech at Mansion House. Talks began between the French and Germans but almost broke down in September and war again seemed probable. But in the end the Germans gave way and in November agreed to recognize French rights in Morocco in return for the cession of two strips of territory in the French Congo.

Wednesday, September 13. Fanny and I on the 11.15 train to Leeds. Tram to Beeston Hill and called at 23, Green Mount Street, to see Mrs Shires, sister of our friend the Rev. Dr. Robt. Collyer. Tea with her and a highly enjoyable two hours talk. Then went to Empire Music Hall for the 6 to 9 performance. Vesta Tilly was the principal turn.

Tuesday, September 19. Met Mr H. Chippendale at Menston re plans. Walked there and back and had three small glasses of Benedictine with Mr. Chippendale. This is a drink distilled by the monks of that Order, so they say.

Monday, September 25. In town in afternoon and paid £12 12*s* to Sinclair and Atkinson re Charles Archer's divorce case.

Friday, September 29. Never in my life did I see so many mushrooms. Look which way you might there they are. All the farmers coming to market had everything full of them, price about one penny per pound. Jonathan off to Bradford with about 40lbs of them.

Friday, October 6. Charles Archer, my nephew, here from Bramhope. He seems to be on his beam ends again. Out of work, has to leave his house, no wife, but three small children, no money. So there is nothing for it but to help him through his trials.

Thursday, October 19. This is the gloomy part of the season when fogs are rife. The autumn tints of the trees are unusually beautiful this fall and the absence of wind causes the leaves to fall like 'gentle dew upon the earth beneath' as Shakespeare or somebody says.

Monday, October 23. Not a very profitable day as regard industry. I feel I should be doing something better than idling time away. I feel as if I should write something of the times and the changes I have seen in life. Maybe I shall do a little in that way sometime.

Thursday, November 9. At Liberal Club reading the papers, mostly about the resignation of Mr Balfour the leader of the Conservative Party.

> *Arthur James Balfour (1848–1930). His habitual unhurried casualness lost him support and he resigned in favour of Andrew Bonar Law (1858–1923)*

Politics is a game where much envy and jealousy prevails and Balfour is too honest a man to stoop to the tricks of party manouevres, though he has done a little at it sometimes. Much talk up at Clifton about a young couple of lovers, George Lister and Miss Priestley who have been inseparable for the past few months and now she has shabbily cast him adrift for another. Woman thy name is frailty.

Sunday, November 12. I am 67 years old today. In good health and hearty. Savoury pudding and roast pork to dinner with apple sauce.

Friday, November 17. Otley Statutes. Very rough wild wet morning. Attendance much below the average. The old lively character of this event is passing away and will be extinct in a few years time. I have seen, say 50 of them, and found them mostly vanity.

Thursday, November 23. Fried bacon and cocoa and white bread to breakfast, then town on shopping errands in a very cold wind. Fried pigs liver, onion and Yorkshire pudding to dinner. Johnny Pennington came with a cart and took all our gooseberry trees as we have not enough room to grow them conveniently. In moderate health but not very robust. Practically teetotal though I took just a little brandy and hot water in the evening, the first for a long time.

Thursday, November 30. Foggy and dark. Our folks have the house apart with Christmas cleaning down, so I went to town and called on Harriet Bushby, nee Spence. She is Timble born and keeps a tea house in Bay Horse Yard. A kipper each to tea. Pancakes to dinner. We are doing rarely.

Friday, December 1. Charles Archer has removed to Yeadon and has now got a job as roadman on the Bramhope sector of roads.

Thursday, December 7. Up to Clifton on Rate business. Much talk about Miss Priestley again. She is a grand-daughter of the late James Lund and appears to be making ducks and drakes of her grandfather's money. Her flirtations and courting escapades are notorious.

Sunday, December 10. Good dinner of roast pork. At 2 p.m. at Wesleyan Chapel to hear *The Messiah.* Very good performance. Miss Nelly Judson, soprano, the best.

Thursday, December 21. Across to town where preparations on all hands for Christmas cheer. However people may cry out about the hard times, and they do cry out as they always did, there seems to be more and more of the good things for everybody. But people are restless and discontented and the more they get the more they want.

Monday, Christmas Day. Up at 8. Nice calm morning. Walked up Newall Carr and on to Weston Moor. Talked with Sam Philips, Sam Barnes, Watty Robinson, Jim Greenwood and others. Home by 1.

Roast sparerib and plum pudding to dinner. Sister Mary Ann arrived just before dinner.

Sunday, December 31. Walked to Sowerby Farm at Timble by noon and there till 5. Fanny came up from Timble and we walked home with the pale moon overhead and in a mild Spring-like air. Thus ended the year.

My brother has retired from farming and now lives in a cosy cottage at Guiseley. My nephew George Archer has got married and my sister Mary Ann has gone to live with her daughter at Sowerby Farm, so I alone of the family am left in harness. We have always retained a hankering hope of some day going back to live Timble way, but the decline of population and social attractions over there begins to make us feel less drawn than we were.

1912

Monday, January 1. The women came down at intervals up to 9 o'clock. We all seem tired after the Christmas and New Year festivities. Remarkably fine and mild. The weather is so uncommon it is the most common subject of talk. No real winter weather yet.

Tuesday, January 2. Fanny and Dorothy and Blanche Thackwray off to Bradford to see the pantomime. Arrived back home about midnight. So that's the way the money goes.

Wednesday, January 3. Town in forenoon on various official work, returns, etc. Very good dinner of roast sparerib and roast potatoes and apple sauce. I find sparerib is much improved by being in salt a week or more.

Friday, January 5. Had a poorish night through bilious indigestion. I have been remarkably immune from this complaint for over a year. I think it is due to eating too much pigs sparerib.

Friday, January 19. Another miserable day. Practically eat nothing. It must end or mend before long. Doctor comes every day. I claimed on the Club. Doctor does not think it dangerous.

Thursday, February 1. Up at 9.30. Cup of cocoa before rising. Fresh boiled egg about 11. A small bit of Yorkshire pudding at dinner time. A little bit of chicken to tea with cocoa and a piece of oatmeal parkin. I like oatmeal in any form. Much better today and trust it may continue.

Monday, February 5. Fanny took my overseers books to the Union offices for audit. She also went to the Workhouse to register a death. She shapes very well and my sickness may be useful in getting her into the way of doing deputy duties.

Saturday, February 10. Improving in health I think. Took 10.54 train to Pool, inspected building and back by 12.16 train. Dinner quite hearty. Afternoon action in garden. Reading Victor Hugo's *Les Miserables.*

Tuesday, February 13. Town in forenoon. Fish to dinner. Appetite has come back and I can eat fairly hearty but I am rather careful what I take. We have a nice easy-going life all along now. Aunt Mary in her 78th year, self in my 69th, Fanny in her 53rd is it? And Dorothy in her 21st. We eat well and argues on various matters and keep from rusting by friction of various sorts.

Saturday, February 17. In town in forenoon. Paid the Co-op 28*s* for 24 cwts of coals. Got shaved and paid 1½*d* for Liberal Club reading papers.

Friday, February 23. Over in town at 12 and dinner at the White Horse. Two glasses of good old port after. Back to town to Mrs Eastwood's who occupied our house in Station Road. She is a very good tenant but is always wanting something doing. I try to humour her as far as I can as tenants are very kittle mettle now in these bad times for property owners.

Wednesday, February 28. Coal strike all the talk today. To what are we drifting?

> The world seems troubled as a whole
> Since colliers gave up getting coal

Sunday, March 3. Shaved, had bath and dressed. Mutton chop to dinner. Reading *Life of Byron* in afternoon and in evening at Ralph Wilson's talking of old times.

Monday, March 4. Up at 6.30. Made my usual dose of porridge and our folks grumble that I use most of the milk. The coal strike is in full blast and the outlook is very gloomy. A sort of revolution seems to be imminent. The Labour Party holds the field.

Wednesday, March 13. Took 10.54 train to Leeds and saw architect and Mr Swift re plans. Dinner at Lockhart's. Four-course dinner for one shilling. Back on 1.23 train.

Wednesday, March 20. A very wild windy sleety morning. The hills are capped with snow. The lambs are coming fast but the season is not good they say. The coal strike blocks the way in everything and a settlement is not yet in view. England is in a fix. She is throttled by the power of organised democracy and she will have to bend to the inevitable. Will she stand the strain without revolution?

Saturday, March 23. Walked with Fanny to Carr Top, she on her way to Timble to teach Sunday School tomorrow. I at home and oatmeal porridge to supper.

Monday., March 29. Slack trade at Lister's auction mart on account of the coal strike they say. We seem to be moving to a new order of society. Whether the change will be carried out in peaceful compromise remains to be seen. The men are now the masters and the know their power. Capital will be compelled to give way to their claims.

Wednesday, March 27. Many families are now run out of coal and none can be had. We have about a fortnight's supply and hope this will see us over the trouble.

The country just now is very upset
And the game will go on as you may bet
The rich man is fearing the Socialist breed
Because they will stop his old grabbing greed

Tuesday, April 2. Scores of people digging coal out of the railway bank between Burley and Otley. It is coal that has been thrown out of the tenders as dirt and refuse for years and now in a time of famine it comes in handy.

Tuesday, April 9. Graving garden in afternoon. I feel I cannot write as freely as formerly. A sort of tremor in my hand.

Wednesday, April 17. All the talk is about the wreck of the *Titanic* with a loss of life which is truly appalling.

Some 1,500 people out of 2,200 passengers were lost when the White Star liner sank on her maiden voyage on the night of April 14–15 after hitting an iceberg in the north Atlantic.

Thursday, April 18. Most beautifully warm day and Nature all looking fresh. My health fairly good. Weighed myself at Bradford Station. Just 10 stones, a few pounds lighter than my normal weight of late years.

Saturday, April 20. Busy day sowing and planting in garden. Put almost all of it in today, potatoes first, then lettuce, onions, parsley and radishes. Fanny and Dorothy went to Timble after tea and will be there all night.

Wednesday, April 24. Writing out Poor Rate all day. Wrote the Rate for both Newall-with-Clifton and Timble Great, both at 2*s* 6*d* in the pound. Helped to shake carpets in the evening. In moderate health all along. Appetite very good. I take oatmeal porridge at least once every day and cocoa usually twice — it suits me better than tea.

> *The obligation to provide help for the poor was first imposed on parishes by the Elizabethan Poor Law of 1601. From 1834 the Poor Rate levied on the estimated value of property, was administered under elected boards of guardians. Workhouses, part of the system, became a social disgrace and were resented especially in the North of England. No able-bodied man received help unless he entered a workhouse. Elected boards of guardians were replaced in 1921 when county or borough councils set up public assistance committees to supervise relief.*

Friday May 3. Plans committee at 11. Most gloriously fine day for Otley Show, but being anything but well I came home and rested. The echo of the Show reached across here but I felt no desire to be there. The motorcars stir up the dust fearfully and all this motor business has sprung up since we came to Otley some 11 or 12 years ago.

Saturday, May 11. Up by 7 and off by early dinner time to Timble. Walked by Dog Park and Low Snowden. Assisted in audit of Club accounts. Also acted as Grand Master at Lodge meeting.

Whit Monday, May 27. Bradford Walk. Over 40 competitors passed here soon after noon. They mostly looked tired and haggard. Public houses in town noisy with drunken fools. Bicycles, motor bikes and motorcars throng the roads. Gentleman and lady called wanting to take a house. They bid £30 a year for ours. Perhaps we had better let as it is too big for us. We shall see.

Friday, May 31. Mrs Powell came with butter and charged 1*s* 8*d* per roll of 24 ounces while the market price was only about 1*s* 4*d*. So Fanny told her to bring no more. Such little frictions do come in this vale of tears.

Just now all Nature looks its best
And Man is now, if ever, blessed
I dare say most will still complain
Some wanting drought and others rain
Still I go on in cheerful mood
I've clothes galore and ample food

Sunday, June 2. A wet day and very few people stirring about. Roast veal and new potatoes to dinner. All of us at Congregational Church in the evening. Later at John Kays. Mr and Mrs Padgett there. Talk on the Bacon–Shakespeare theory. Padgett is deep in these things.

Monday, June 3. The wettest day of the year. At it all day. All is saturated.

Friday, June 7. Made out two certificates of deaths and registered a birth. Seven shillings in fees the result. This is the best source of income there is connected with my appointment.

Thursday, June 13. Train to Ilkley and inspected building in progress on the Middleton site. Tea at a cafe in Brook Street and 6.15 train back home. The summer is now putting on its meridian dress of many lines with its sweet scents. Life is prolific on every hand and the air blows it among the trees and the fields waken to the impulse. Life rustles among the shady leaves of the woods and resounds in a thousand voices of bird and beast. Yet amongst it all Death stalks along snatching his victims.

Saturday, June 15. A very rainy time. The farmers have had more than enough of it and week-enders are disgusted. Still it is a growing time. The Engineers Band of Music played selections in Manor Square in the evening but were broken off before completing their programme.

Thursday, June 20. Took 1.6 train to Leeds, then to Alwoodley by tram and inspected foundations of new houses. Back to Leeds and in Moving Picture Gallery for an hour. Very wonderful. Good tea at Collinsons Cafe. Strolled through market and bought one pound of very fine strawberries, price fourpence. Took 8.15 train home.

Thursday, July 4. Home and around most of the day. In moderate health all along, only I feel to be getting older and feels as if I wanted to leave off the worry of the routine of duty. Still, so long as I can do it without any great strain or difficulty I keep going and trust by

God's blessing to keep matters decent and in order. Yet the time cannot be far off when I will have to vacate the offices I now fill either voluntarily or by pressure of years or something.

Saturday, July 6. Women busy cleaning up in forenoon. I was busy in the garden up to 4 p.m. Made all very smart. The lawn and the flowers are very much admired by passers-by. We certainly keep our garden in better order than most.

Sunday, July 7. Up at 8. Fine summers day. Lamb and green peas to dinner. Ascended summit of the Chevin in the evening. Very fine view but tiring work.

Monday, July 8. Close and warm. The ground is drying out and haytime just getting into swing. The National Insurance Act is the main talk all along. Lloyd George comes in for terrible abuse, but when he speaks he floors them all.

Britain's National Insurance Act of 1911 added unemployment to the scope of social insurance designed to protect wage-earners and their dependents from economic hazards.

Friday, July 12. George Archer, William Pennington and I met Mr Renwick at Walkers, the printers, re arranging transference of the Timble Club to the Oddfellows Order for the purposes of the Insurance Act.

Monday, July 15. Terribly close hot day and all that could be desired for the hay. Crops very heavy and given fine weather the farmers hearts will rejoice. I feel upset with this heat and keeps quiet indoors mostly. My feet are in bad order for walking and I have a bit of rheumatism in my legs so I am in no form for knocking about. I feel as if my days of intense action are over and if I remain on the stage I shall have to take an easy part and try to keep out of the way of others.

Wednesday, July 17. In fair health all along but has to be careful what I eat.

Friday, July 19. Up at 7.30. Dull weather. Came on wet towards night. In town after dinner. Few farmers in the market as the haytime is on. Evening with George Holmes an hour talking old times over.

Saturday, July 20. Not very well this morning. Up with Ralph Wilson who was mowing with a scythe in the forenoon. I registered a birth and also a death and made out five certificates for the deaths at 2*s* 6*d* each so that was a good haul. Mr and Mrs Kay here in the evening and later Mr and Mrs Alfred Marshall called. I was far from well. My old catarrh of the stomach.

Sunday, July 21. Only a poor night. Up at 11 but ate nothing at all all day. Most miserable time. Dull cloudy weather. This is very depressing, but I hope as usual.

The diary is continued by a different hand. It is Fanny's. It is a bold and buxom script as the brief glimpses of her have led a reader to imagine herself to be. The language — except for a single and momentary outbreak of emotion — is also a reflection of the diarist's rare references to her ways in 23 years of marriage: spare and forthright.

Monday, July 22. My husband was taken seriously ill on Sunday night. Never free from pain all night. Nothing seemed to relieve it. Fetched Dr Williamson again on Monday morning. Ordered a nurse and injections. Was easier during the day. Had to have nothing all day.

Tuesday, July 23. Had a good night so nurse said. Doctor came and thought him a little better in some respects but advised a specialist. Brought Dr Thompson back with him from Leeds and by his advice he was taken to Leeds Infirmary about 3 o'clock in the afternoon. My husband was quite reconciled to go if that was the only way. Sat up in bed and told me what to do if anything should happen. Signed cheques and told Dorothy, his only child, a young woman, 'to be a good girl till he came back.'

Wednesday, July 24. 3 p.m. a ring at the front door bell to tell me and Dorothy to go at once to Leeds Infirmary. Got up at once and dressed and went to Waites and ordered a taxicab to take us to Leeds. Arrived there about 6 p.m. Too late. Life had almost fled. Did not know us. O, the bitterness of grief. Will the clouds ever lift or the sun shine again?

My husband was one of Nature's gentlemen, an honest man who tried to do to others as he would be done by, and now he has gone to his Maker to give an account of the deeds done in the body.

Thursday, July 25. Went to Leeds this morning with G. Archer and his wife and Dorothy to get my husband's death certificate at the Infirmary. Duodenal ulcer was on it. Perforation. So that accounts for all the pain on Sunday night. I shall always think his life might have been saved could something have been done on Sunday night unless there is an appointed time for each to die. Got mourning in Leeds. Felt a painful business. Arrived home about 6 o'clock. My husband was brought home about an hour later.

Friday, July 26. Callers kept coming all day. Everybody is kind and full of sympathy. Getting ready for the funeral. Rather unsettled weather. Mrs Archer, John's sister, is with us. My good old mother is a wonderful help and stay to us although 78 years of age. Her mind is very bright and clear. She has known much sorrow and trouble. She has lived with us about six years.

Saturday, July 27. Up betimes this morning. Started off with the funeral from here about half past one p.m. Mr Handyside, the Wesleyan Minister, came up to read and say a few words. It began to rain as we went up Newall Carr. Had a thunderstorm on the moors and another when we got to Timble. Had to wait half an hour, then journeyed on to Fewston new cemetery where he had rather wished to be buried. The rain then began to come down in torrents like emptying buckets on the cabs. When we arrived at the cemetery all was in flood. It had filled the grave and we could not inter. The oldest inhabitants never had seen it rain so fast.

Sunday, July 28. Another thunderstorm today almost as bad as yesterday. The country is all flooded.

Monday, July 29. Interred my husband this morning at 11 a.m. Could not do it before owing to the heavy rains.

Ronald Harker was born in 1909 in Grassington, North Yorkshire, where his family has been settled for centuries. He has been a journalist all his working life, saw army service in India and on Earl Mountbatten's South–East Asia headquarters staff in Ceylon, and returned to Fleet Street as Night Editor of the *News Chronicle.* He joined the *Observer* in 1956 as Night Editor and Editor of its Foreign News Service. He paid several visits to the Middle East, wrote *Digging Up The Bible Lands* in 1972, and has since retired to his native village.